nothing is impossible

STORIES THAT ARE BEYOND BELIEF

BARBARA JOINER

Woman's Missionary Union
Birmingham, Alabama

Woman's Missionary Union
P. O. Box 830010
Birmingham, AL 35283-0010

For more information, visit our Web site at www.wmu.com or
call 1-800-968-7301.

Dewey Decimal Classification: 231.7
Subject Headings: PROVIDENCE AND GOVERNMENT OF GOD
                  MIRACLES—CHRISTIANITY
                  MISSIONARY STORIES

    Scripture quotations marked KJV are from the King James
Version.
    Scripture quotations from *The Message*. Copyright ©1991,
1994, 1995. Used by permission.
    Scripture quotations marked NASB are from the NEW AMER-
ICAN STANDARD BIBLE ®, © Copyright The Lockman Foundation 1960, 1962, 1963, 1968, 1971, 1972, 1973, 1975, 1977. Used
by permission.
    Scripture quotations identified NIV are from the Holy Bible,
New International Version. Copyright ©1973, 1978, 1984 International Bible Society. Used by permission of Zondervan Bible
Publishers.

Photo credits: Brand X Pictures and PhotoDisc
Cover design by Janell Young

ISBN: 1-56309-951-9
W053107•1004•1.5M2

Contents

Dedication

I dedicate this to my first editor, the late William Joseph (Joe) Smith—my dear, beloved friend.

BJ

Introduction

I believe in miracles. Always have; always will. The fact that *Beyond Belief!*, vol. 2 is in your hands is one of the biggest miracles of my life.

I was excited about this book. It was the first professional collaboration of editor William Joseph Smith and Barbara Joiner.

Joe had joined Woman's Missionary Union® in 1997 as design editor of *Dimension* and other WMU® resources. Within days of turning on his computer, he called me to set up our first book.

Alas, I couldn't do it until 2000, but we set it up.

I mentioned it was to be our first professional collaboration. You see, Joe grew up in Columbiana, Alabama, my hometown. His dad says he grew up in the Joiner household, and he did. Our whole family loved Joe.

It was not until our youth group had a creative retreat that I discovered his talents with the written word. That weekend each person in the group could choose drama, music, art, or writing. Our minister of music and youth asked me to lead the writing seminar. I was underwhelmed. But Joe and half the football team chose writing, which caused all the cheerleaders to choose writing.

We had a ball in that seminar, and many in the group wrote some good stuff. Joe's was great! We ended up writing a devotional booklet during the weekend and presented it to all the campers.

I encouraged Joe's writing from that point on. And I was a proud "mama" when he gave his craft to the Lord and to WMU.

Then in 1999, Joe started having some problems. When the doctors checked him, they found he needed open-heart surgery immediately. They operated on November 17. It did not go well. His heart stopped on the operating table. They started it back, but damage had been done.

We watched and prayed. He held his own for a while. On November 18, Joe's wife, Nancy, asked me to go in with her on the last visit of the night. After hugs and kisses, Joe reminded me that we were to meet about the book on Monday, November 22.

"I'll be home by then," he promised.

And he was. He went to be with the Father the next day, November 19. He was only 39. He left his wife, Nancy, and two precious children, Jake and Julie.

And me, with a hole in my heart.

Finally, on February 22, I had my first meeting with the new editor, Nell Branum. We decided that the first chapter should be completed and all research done by June 1.

Beyond belief, that chapter was in Nell's hands before we left for migrant camp. I had also completed a mountain of research.

Migrant camp—usually the joy of my life—was tragic. One of our boys, Terry White, drowned.

The hole in my heart got bigger.

I asked the Lord to give me back my joy and to help me write the next chapter—already due. I struggled. But I did walk and not faint, and dreamed of mounting up with eagles again some day.

The enemy knew he had me down for the count. So he added a few "now do you give ups?"—such as hemorrhaging retinas and skin cancer right between my eyes. But prayer and two fine doctors patched me right up.

Finally, I was writing again. Every friend I have was praying without ceasing. Wonderful material flooded my mailbox. I wrote on tray tables on airplanes and on kitchen tables in Hawaii, plus 15 other states.

I finished chapters 2 and 3 and kept going. I finished, thank the good Lord, I finished! It's a miracle beyond belief! And the hole in my heart is not so big anymore.

The Great Escape

The song by Oscar C. Eliason asks: "Got any rivers you think are uncrossable?" God's resounding answer is "Nothing . . . is impossible with God" (Luke 1:37 *The Message*).

Four impossible escapes claim this chapter. They represent the tip of the iceberg, for God specializes in things that seem impossible—such as escapes that are beyond belief.

THE FIRST GREAT ESCAPE

Matthew (not his real name) lived in Sudan in northeast Africa. Sudan is the largest nation in Africa—larger than all of the United States east of the Mississippi River. A vicious civil war rages in the country, leaving millions dead or suffering. Murder, rape, slave-taking, and kidnapping are commonplace.

Northern Sudan, populated by fundamentalist Muslims, want an Islamic state. The South, with a strong Christian influence, fought against such a state. Matthew lived deep in southern Sudan. It was quiet. But one night, while sitting and talking with his father, his whole compound filled with soldiers who began shooting. They shot Matthew's father.

"I could not control myself," remembers Matthew. He tried to take a gun from one of the soldiers. He was captured and taken away to a military prison.

It was a descent into a kind of hell. Matthew describes the beatings and the torture—every morning, every night. After a couple of weeks of beatings and burning, he could no longer feel the pain—even the pain in his injured, swollen leg.

"You cannot really feel if you are a human being," Matthew laments.

After six months of imprisonment and beatings, something happened. A soldier came and put Matthew and some other prisoners in a larger room in another building. This was better than his former room, which had been a box in which Matthew could neither lie down nor stand up. It was miserable, for Matthew was a big man, just 32 years old.

As Matthew was led to his new quarters, he saw a drainage ditch that ran under the prison wall. Beyond the prison wall was the Nile River.

Matthew asked the guard where the ditch led. The soldier said, "Why do you ask about this water?"

Matthew replied that he was afraid that the putrid water might cause malaria. The guard laughed, "You're already a dead man! You don't have to worry about malaria. You're going to die anyway." Then the guard added that an electric fence would electrocute anyone who tried to escape.

That evening as the men were marched to the kitchen building, when no one seemed to be looking, Matthew limped to the ditch and slipped into the disgusting sewage. He floated. He thinks he floated under the electric fence, unconscious. When he came to, he was on the bank of the Nile.

He hurt all over and could barely breathe from pain. His badly injured leg throbbed. He was weak from hunger. He moved quietly and weakly in the grasses along the riverbank, hiding from the patrolling soldiers who would shoot him on sight.

Then he saw the two bright, yellow eyes, level with his and coming straight at him—a huge Nile crocodile! Then, unbelievably, the crocodile, with a mighty thrust of his giant tail, turned and swam away!

Matthew swallowed the scream in his throat, and softly floated in the bulrushes. He followed the river north, passing military installations and checkpoints. Surely God swam alongside! He floated maybe four days, maybe more. He's not sure.

Exhausted, he clambered up the bank and crawled into the forest. He rested and found fruit, his first food in many days.

For three and a half months, Matthew walked. He avoided any towns or people. Finally, he reached the port of Sudan. He wanted to board a freighter, but without money, further escape seemed impossible. A freighter captain demanded an exorbitant fee. As he pleaded with the man, a priest approached.

Like the Good Samaritan, the priest took Matthew to a room to clean up. Matthew was filthy from months of hiding and running.

The kindly man also helped Matthew book passage on a ship, and Matthew soon found himself in Bulgaria in eastern Europe. It was in Bulgaria that Matthew came face-to-face with Jesus.

An Ethiopian befriended him and took him to a church, International Baptist Church in Sofia. The pastor spoke about loving one's enemies. Matthew scoffed to himself, "I cannot forgive the Arabs who killed my father!"

Then something unusual happened. Twice in a dream Matthew's father appeared to him. "You're always to come in love, not hatred," said his father in the dream. "If you love me, never hate anybody."

James Duke, the Southern Baptist pastor of the church in Sofia, very wisely showed Matthew the

Jesus film. Matthew was astounded that this Jesus was beaten and tortured. He was killed! But He forgave those who did it to Him. Matthew's tears fell. His heart was softened. That day Matthew accepted Jesus as his Savior.

James Duke discipled his new convert. Matthew became actively involved in the church. He was excited about sharing his faith. James encouraged him to go to seminary. Matthew plans to finish seminary, but he has already made other important plans. His escape from Sudan was beyond belief, but he wants to return to his homeland. "We don't know about God in Sudan. We don't know Who Jesus is. I want to go tell them," he beams.

Matthew's great escape will mean freedom for many from the bondage of sin. That is the greatest escape of all.

THE SECOND GREAT ESCAPE

Same river—the mighty Nile that flows through Sudan, through Egypt, into the Mediterranean Sea. Many centuries before Matthew hid in its bulrushes, another made his escape in the Nile's luxuriant growth.

The first two chapters of Exodus set the stage for the second great escape. The children of Israel were in Egypt and "were fruitful and increased greatly, and multiplied, and became exceedingly mighty, so that the land was filled with them" (Ex. 1:7 NASB).

It had all started with Joseph who was sold into slavery by his own brothers (Gen. 37:27). Then he was sold to Pharaoh's bodyguard.

God was with Joseph, and he eventually became second only to Pharaoh in Egypt. When famine almost wiped out his family in Canaan, he was able to save them from starvation. His family settled in

Egypt and prospered. Joseph died, and eventually another Pharaoh came to power "who did not know Joseph" (Ex. 1:8). All this new Pharaoh could see were Hebrews everywhere. He tried to work them to death, but the more he afflicted them, the more they multiplied.

The great construction schemes under the lash of Egyptian taskmasters produced the pyramids and mighty fortresses. Still the Israelites increased.

Then Pharaoh decreed a heartbreaking law: "Every [Hebrew] son who is born you are to cast into the Nile" (Ex. 1:22).

Can you imagine the horror of the expectant mothers? Of course, if the child were a girl, she would be spared.

Chapter 2 of Exodus introduces us to a husband and wife caught in this horrible dilemma. In Exodus 6:20 we learn their names—Amram and Jochebed. They already had a daughter, Miriam, and a son, Aaron. Then Jochebed found herself growing heavy with another child.

Jochebed surely had recognized the signs early on, having borne two children already. And she knew, as did all the Hebrew women, how meticulously and ruthlessly Pharaoh charted the Hebrew births. Grief could easily be her lot.

My first child was born during the thalidomide scare. This drug was prescribed to expectant mothers for nausea. When the babies of these mothers were born, some were disfigured. Arms were missing, legs were missing, there were other problems.

I had not taken the drug, but my mind was twisted with fear. After my child was born, I frantically reached for my little girl and counted every finger and toe, ran my hands over each tiny arm and leg, and I cried in relief and joy.

My fear was in small measure compared to the fear of the Israelite women. Imagine Jochebed's broken question to the midwife, "What is it?" And the answer, like a piercing arrow: "It's a boy."

Her heart must have stopped. Then a fierce determination filled her being. She determined that her child would not die! No wave or hungry crocodile would claim her son.

Jochebed saw that "he was beautiful" (Ex. 2:2). Acts 7:20 declares that he was fair to God. Could it be that Jochebed felt a little one sent from God lay in her lap? Could she have somehow sensed that God had a special plan for Moses? Who would have believed he would grow up to be the deliverer of his people! Abraham Kuyper says: "[Jochebed's] faith mingled with her love, and, armed with these, she determined at whatever price it might be to rescue her baby."[1]

We don't know what happened in the following three months. We can only imagine that Jochebed hid little Moses away in a corner of the house or maybe the stable where he had air, but could not be easily heard. We can see her slipping away to nurse the baby and love him.

She knew the hiding could not go on forever. Moses was growing and he cried and laughed lustily.

Then Jochebed devised a plan. She made an ark, a basket of sorts. She waterproofed it with tar and pitch (Ex. 2:3). How many kisses she must have rained on that dear little face as she placed him in the basket and lowered him into the water! She charged her daughter, Miriam, to keep watch over her brother.

Miriam was up to the task. She kept a sharp eye on the basket. She probably checked to be sure that it stayed dry inside and that the baby was dry as well. She was ready for anything that happened.

Jochebed had placed her child in the bathing pool of Pharaoh's daughter. When she came to bathe, she saw the basket and sent her maids to get it (Ex. 2:5). She opened the basket and saw the child. She was not foolish. She knew at once that it was a Hebrew child, but her heart was touched by the beautiful baby. She must have also known that her father would be furious with her if she defied his law and did not drown the child immediately. But her heart refused to abandon him. Escape comes from strange quarters!

At this point, Miriam stepped forward. "Shall I go and call a nurse for you from the Hebrew women, that she may nurse the child for you?" (Ex. 21:7).

Pharaoh's daughter accepted Miriam's offer, and Miriam brought to the princess her own ecstatic mother, the baby's own mother, Jochebed.

Not only did the princess ask Jochebed to nurse the babe until he was older, but she actually paid her for doing the joyous task.

Jochebed had precious time with Moses where she could love him and teach him. She also secured his future in the very palace of Pharaoh. For when Moses was older, she returned him to the princess, who gave him the life of a prince.

The escape of Moses from certain death is beyond belief! But no more so than the escape of the children of Israel out of bondage in Egypt, led by their awesome leader who was once scooped from the River Nile.

God specializes in things that seem impossible!

THE THIRD GREAT ESCAPE

One more river: the swift-flowing, deadly Mekong in southeast Asia. On one side was Communist-dominated Laos. One mile across was Thailand and freedom.

Many had made this passage to freedom, using every means possible, from banana tree trunks to inflatable tubes. If you had money, you could hire a mercenary to carry you over in his speedboat—if you were willing to dodge a few bullets.

Some made it to safety and freedom. Some did not. One who did is Victor.

Victor was born in 1966, the year of the horse according to the Chinese calendar. His delivery required two midwives and a medicine man. Victor was the sixth of eight children. He was born in Savannahkhet, Laos.

All of southeast Asia trembled under Communist attack. The Vietnam War was at the boiling point. Savannahkhet was a real target because of its strong military base.

"My mother has a strong will and great courage," observes Victor. She practically raised the children by herself since her husband was in the military. Every day she got the children to school and then went to the market where she was a merchant. That was how she supported her family.

As the political unrest grew, some of the children went to live with their grandparents in the country on a rice farm. At age 6 or 7, Victor went to his grandparents' farm. He worked hard. He also got to know his grandfather, who was a devout Buddhist. As Victor talked with his grandfather, he could not help but wonder about a Supreme Being.

One day, when Victor was halfway through third grade, he was walking to school when his mother called out to him and told him to be silent and to come with her. She dressed Victor in three or four layers of clothing although it was very hot. As they walked to the market, she explained to her little boy that he was crossing the Mekong to meet his father in Thailand. She had cleverly arranged to hire a merchant who would claim Victor as his son and take him across the river using false identification papers.

Victor felt all alone for the crossing. It was too risky for more than one family member to cross at a time. Can you imagine a little third-grader making such a journey?

Victor remembers crying during the crossing. He wondered if he'd ever see his mother again. He had been told to go through customs and inspections when they landed. Would they discover he was trying to escape? However, all went smoothly, and his father was there to meet him.

Little did they realize that it would take three years before the family would all be safely out of Laos.

As the family members trickled into Thailand, they were placed in a refugee camp. Victor declares that he grew out of his childhood quickly. His mother, an ardent Buddhist, decided to put young Victor in a Buddhist monastery to become a monk. Even there, seeds of hope began to scatter in his empty soul. Victor whispers, "Now I realize that God knew me even before I was born."

After waiting in the refugee camp for two years, Victor's family was chosen to relocate in America. A Christian family and church in Seaford, Virginia, sponsored them.

Victor watched how those Christians lived with so much love. Then he went to a Backyard Bible Club. He admits that it was mostly for the food and games. However, the experience brought him closer to God.

When Victor was 14 he accepted Christ as his Savior. He was baptized the following year. One of his chief encouragers was his Sunday School teacher, Tom Hunter, who was helping with the Laotian ministry in Montgomery, Alabama, where the family had moved. Tom was an alumnus of Samford University in Birmingham. It was Victor's dream to go to Samford. But he was not academically eligible, nor was he financially able.

He went instead to a technical college in Montgomery, studying drafting and drawing. "I got bored drawing straight lines and no coloring," Victor laughs.

He transferred to Auburn University at Montgomery and immediately became totally involved in missions: summer missions, spring break missions. He also discovered his gifts in photography. "A picture is worth a thousand words," he declares. And Victor's pictures are, indeed!

Tom Hunter asked Victor, "Are you ready to go to Samford yet?" Then he took Victor to Birmingham to see the campus.

"I fell in love with the beautiful campus," Victor remembers, "and they were playing my game—soccer!"

Tom took Victor to registration where all things were worked out beyond belief! Another river was crossed when Victor entered Samford in the fall of 1990.

With graduation near, Victor interviewed with the Woman's Missionary Union®, national office, where he served as the graphic designer for *Our Missions World*, *Nuestra Tarea*, and other language products for more than five years.

Another stellar happening was his meeting beautiful Susan, who is now Mrs. Victor. Susan is Amerasian with an American father and a Korean mother. Like Victor, she is a fine, committed Christian.

In November 2000, Victor and Susan boarded an airplane that would take them to their new assignment as IMB personnel. The place? Thailand! Though these are not their real names, their story is true.

That little third-grader, whose great escape involved crossing the Mekong River into Thailand, is going back to its very banks to share the love of Jesus. That is beyond belief!

THE FOURTH GREAT ESCAPE

The word *escape* is not a word we associate with the United States. This is the land of the free, the land of opportunity, a bastion of Christianity.

Yet treacherous rivers abound for some. The rapids of poverty pull countless people under. Tides of ignorance sweep over hundreds of hapless victims. The quicksands of circumstance suck the very life from scores of struggling people.

For women such as these—and most of the victims are women—Christian Women's Job Corps® was created by Woman's Missionary Union®.

Since its beginning, CWJC℠ has met the needs of thousands of women. The ministry, primarily led by volunteers, empowers women in their moves from welfare to economic independence in a Christian context.

CWJC is a life-skills and job-readiness program that equips women with skills that will help them secure and actually do a job satisfactorily. Volunteers teach and encourage. They serve as mentors, provide childcare, furnish transportation, teach the Bible, cook meals, sort used clothing, answer phones, and pray. The list is amazing, and one of the volunteer jobs will fit *you* like a glove! Will you give a hand? Contact your state WMU office for information about the CWJC site nearest you. Talk to the site coordinator about becoming a volunteer.

A Sheryl Barrett may be waiting for you to help her escape.

Sheryl lives in Rock Hill, South Carolina, which is in York County. Thank goodness, York County has a

CWJC site, and it's in Rock Hill, because Sheryl was in need of help.

Sheryl's mentor, Laura Cook, describes her first meeting with Sheryl: "I first met Sheryl three years ago on a hot August afternoon. She [was] 45 years old, had finished seventh grade, had never worked, had never learned to drive, and had no social skills. She spoke loudly in a monotone voice and never made eye contact. From the time she had left school in the seventh grade until I met her, she had not been allowed to leave home. Her father was very controlling and had only allowed her to go to the grocery store with her mom."

Laura continues telling about that first sad visit. She discovered that the little mobile home also housed Sheryl's 47-year-old brother, who also had only finished the seventh grade, and her 73-year-old mother. Her father had died the year before. Oh yes, the trailer was also home for six cats and four dogs.

Laura remembers being suffocated by the odors that hot afternoon. Later she called Elizabeth Ford, the CWJC site coordinator, to ask what Elizabeth expected her to do.

Elizabeth's response was classic. First, she said she didn't know what needed to be done or where to start. Then she said, "Whatever you do will be a success because right now there is nothing . . . no hope in her life."

Laura could have run. She could have said that she didn't have the time or energy. She could have named all the things she was already doing in her local church.

Instead, she started meeting with Sheryl weekly. They began with Bible study. When Sheryl discovered through the Scriptures that God loved her, her amazement was heartlifting!

Sheryl also started setting goals. The top goal was a better place to live.

Together Laura and Sheryl developed a plan to reach that goal:
1. Get a job.
2. Learn to drive.
3. Get a car.
4. Take the GED examination.

Does all that sound impossible for a "homebound" woman? Could Sheryl escape from four decades of grinding poverty?

But never before had Sheryl had a mentor and friend like Laura Cook! Never before had she had Christian Women's Job Corps! Never before had she had the God of the impossible!

Of course she could escape!

When it was time for her first job interview, Laura spent days role-playing with Sheryl, instructing her to make eye contact, sit up straight, talk in an "inside" voice, and ask appropriate questions. Over and over they practiced.

Now Sheryl has held her job as a maid at a local hotel for over two years. "Dependable, hardworking, and trustworthy" are the evaluations of her employer.

Elizabeth Ford cannot say enough about Sheryl's progress. She boasts that Sheryl has completed and graduated from everything York County CWJC has suggested to help her become self-sufficient. She has graduated from a vocational rehabilitation program. She has graduated from an introduction to computers offered by an adult education program. She has finished every class and life-skill group she has been asked to complete. She has also completed every Bible study—one a week—and has become a part of this ministry.

Elizabeth proudly points to "so many firsts" in Sheryl's life: riding a bus, going somewhere without her mother, going to a park, to a mall, to a fast-food restaurant.

Sheryl owns her first Bible, her first pocketbook. She got her first professional haircut. She's gone to a doctor and a dentist.

"Watching Sheryl," says Elizabeth, "has been like watching a cactus turn into a rose, one petal at a time. To hear her laugh now is like hearing angels sing!"

But nobody knows Sheryl the way Laura Cook does. Her memories are priceless. She remembers "showing [Sheryl] what the Bible says about eternal life." She remembers Sheryl's prayer to receive Jesus as her Savior, and the instant hope that was in her eyes after that prayer.

It was no easy step for Sheryl to walk down the aisle and publicly tell of her decision. It was even more difficult to actually follow through with the baptism. She called Laura the evening of the baptism to say that she couldn't do it, she'd drown.

Laura's husband and sons got on their knees and prayed while Laura calmed Sheryl. That night Laura stood behind Sheryl in the baptismal pool.

Laura remembers all the days they spent learning to drive, and she recalls the jubilation of Sheryl getting her driver's license. She remembers the car someone donated for Sheryl. God is so good!

His goodness and generosity continues. Going by to pick Sheryl up for church one evening, Laura found her with a horribly abscessed tooth. Sheryl had always pulled her own teeth, which left some problems. Laura took Sheryl to a dentist who gave her antibiotics and talked to an oral surgeon, who did all the complicated extractions and follow-up free of charge. The dentist also made dentures—free of charge.

Sheryl continues to work full-time, work on her GED, and save money for a down payment on a small home.

In June 2000, the Woman's Missionary Union Foundation awarded Sheryl one of the first two grants ever given from the new Sybil Bentley Dove Endowment Fund.

The $250 award will be added to her nest egg. Please God, let it be enough for that down payment, that final boost across the abyss of poverty. That escape will be beyond belief!

Got any rivers that seem to be uncrossable? God specializes in things that seem impossible—beyond belief!

[1] Abraham Kuyper, *Women of the Old Testament* (Grand Rapids, MI: Zondervan, 1961), 56.

2

And They Shall Eat and Be Satisfied

In 1984 I went to Nigeria as part of the partnership between Nigeria and Alabama. I led prayer retreats from one end of that wonderful country to the other. In between the prayer retreats, which were for the Southern Baptist missionaries, I spoke anywhere—and I do mean anywhere—the missionaries wanted me to speak. I spoke at the American Wives' Club in Lagos, in bush churches in the jungles, at the hostel for missionaries' kids in Jos. But one of my very favorite places was the Baptist seminary in Kaduna.

For five weeks I traveled in Nigeria. I ate many new foods. I liked them all. I ate and was satisfied. I needed not one antacid to aid digestion. Of course, my missionary hosts and hostesses took good care of me.

I remember that on the day of my arrival Southern Baptist missionary Anita Roper explained that all sorts of food could be purchased from the swarms of street vendors.

"Do not even think about it!" she commanded. To emphasize her point, she clapped her hands as a vendor thrust a smoked fish, which was threaded onto a stick, toward her. The clap caused dozens of flies to leave their perches on the fish! I got the message.

Anita added, "You would die!"

OK, OK, I got the message.

When I finally made my way up-country to Kaduna, I was welcomed by Payton Myers, who was then principal of the seminary. He said, "How about doing a dramatic piece in chapel tomorrow? Our students would love that."

"A dramatic piece? What kind of dramatic piece? Thank you very much for the prior notification!" my mind screamed.

Before I could register my frantic objections, one of the missionaries asked, "But who could interpret for her?"

Payton replied confidently, "Oh, Rev. Aboki will."

My mind was desperately searching for any possible drama I could do.

All at once, I remembered a "star-caliber" drama I had seen the year before. Jeanette Clift George had portrayed Stephen's wife—before, during, and after his stoning. It was riveting and heartbreaking.

Don't ever ask me to attempt this feat in the US! But I was desperate. And who in Kaduna, Nigeria, would have seen the famed Jeanette Clift George?

Rev. Aboki came to consult with me. Oh, my! What a gracious, dignified man. It was obvious that we were *not* "two peas in a pod!"

I dove right in. "I am going to tell the story of Stephen's wife," I explained.

"The Stephen that was stoned?" Rev. Aboki asked.

"Yes," I assured him.

"There is not much in the Bible about him," he remarked.

"I know—just in chapters 6 and 7 in Acts. I want you to begin the drama by reading the last three verses of chapter 7."

"There is nothing in my Bible about Stephen's wife," he reminded me.

"I know," I sighed. "I am going to *pretend*."

Rev. Aboki nodded his head. Concern was written on his face.

"If I scream, you scream. If I cry, you cry. If I fall to the floor, you fall." I was becoming very apprehensive.

The students poured into the chapel—women on one side, men on the other.

The women began to sing and accompany themselves on jugs! It was wonderful!

Rev. Aboki and I went to the platform. Rev. Aboki read the Scripture. Then I began telling the story of Stephen's wife. I begged Stephen not to go to preach. He had been warned. Saul himself had been seen going to the marketplace and he hated Christians. I sank to my knees, begging.

Rev. Aboki matched my words with great passion. My every movement was copied exactly.

As the story climaxed, I was distraught and in tears. Rev. Aboki joined me, weeping bitterly.

The students were enthralled. They stood to their feet, cheering.

Payton Myers pulled me to my feet saying, "Barbara, that was great, but Rev. Aboki, you were magnificent!"

And he was! It was the performance of a lifetime! It was beyond belief!

We went from the chapel to faculty break. As I was accepting accolades that really belonged to Rev. Aboki, the "star" hurried into the room and came to me. He had gone to the street and purchased a special snack for himself and me. He handed me a smoked fish threaded onto a stick. He reached into his deep pocket and pulled out a handful of Nigerian "hush puppies"—actually they were *kosai*, which are bean cakes fried in coconut oil.

Anita Roper's face appeared before my eyes as did her words of warning. However, the dear face of my interpreter and new friend, John Aboki, blotted out Anita's face. I accepted the fish and *kosai*. They were both delicious! I ate and was satisfied.

That night my hostess, missionary Faye Burkwall, watched me anxiously. During the night, I heard her tiptoeing to my bedside. But neither flies on the fish nor gutter water in the *kosai* brought me distress. That was, according to the Nigerian missionaries, beyond belief. One missionary said, "Barbara, you must have a cast-iron stomach like Payton Myers!"

IS THAT EYEBALL EYEBALLING ME?

After my Nigerian adventure, I tried to be a little more careful. But I've always been curious and most everything looks and smells delicious to me.

I came to a screeching halt, however, in 1992. I went to Bangladesh to follow in the footsteps of missionary Gloria Thurman for a month. Then I was to return home and write her biography.

Writing about Gloria was a thrill. Visiting Gloria and her husband, Tom, in Bangladesh was a dream come true.

There were, however, two flies in the ointment. The first was the prospect of wearing a *sari* every day. I had tried, many times, to wear a *sari*—six yards of silky material wrapped around and around my body. I had never managed to keep my *sari* up.

My other concern was curry. The slightest whiff of curry has always done me in.

My second day in Bangladesh, however, let me know I had much more to fear than curry. Gloria and I went to call on a brand-new bride and groom in the home of the bride's mother-in-law. We were served a bowl of rice with freshly prepared curry sauce on top.

God sustained me. It also helped that Gloria gave me a "you-hang-in-there" look.

As I held my bowl with trembling fingers, I glanced down and found a special surprise on top of my bowl.

I had not been told that the guest of honor's bowl was garnished with a fish head! I was guest of honor through no merit of my own. I was honored because I was a friend of the Thurmans! Oh, thank you, Tom and Gloria!

There on top of my bowl was an entire small, dried fish. It had little beady eyes and they were fixed on me!

No one was looking, so I pushed it to the bottom of my bowl. About that time a greeting was heard at the door. Two ambitious young men who were trying to learn English had heard that an *exotic* woman was in town, and they wished to converse with me!

So we conversed. And as we talked, I put bits of my rice and curry into my mouth. Then I remembered my fish and searched for it. It was gone. I had eaten it! Let me tell you, if you must eat a small dried fish, that is the way to eat it—without knowing!

I survived that little incident with no ill effects. But I did ask the Thurmans if this gesture could be expected again.

"Yes," was the solemn answer.

"Isn't there any way to skip this thoughtful gesture?" I asked with quivering lips (and liver).

Tom Thurman simply shrugged his shoulders. He turned his back to me. I suspected he was smiling from ear to ear!

The following day we walked miles and miles into my favorite village in Bangledesh, Hatbaria.

The women were already cooking rice when we arrived. Gloria whipped out her pocketknife and began peeling onions for the curry sauce.

I chose the better part. I decided to play with the precious children. I even taught them the chorus, "Deep and Wide."

Too soon, we were called for the meal. We sat on grass mats and were served steaming bowls of rice and curry sauce. A beautiful young woman proudly placed my bowl in my hands. Only the Lord stopped my cry of disbelief. Draped across the top of my bowl was an enormous fish head. It had whiskers! It had eyes as big as marbles and they were "eyeballing" me!

In my heart I cried out to the Lord: "Oh, Lord, You know my heart. I want to eat that fish head, but . . . oh, Lord, You know my stomach and it is neither willing nor capable! I need you NOW!"

As I said "Amen" I heard the most beautiful sound: "MEOW!"

I swiveled my head over my shoulder and saw a big, beautiful tomcat. I knew that cat! God had heard my prayer and had sent His house cat!

OK, I know that's beyond belief. But let me tell you why I know he was God's house cat. I palmed that fish head and swung around. That cat absolutely inhaled the fish head! I mean, he was a high-powered vacuum cleaner. Now, ordinary cats don't do that. They play with their food. They bury it and dig it up—over and over.

But God's house cat was there to help me. He got rid of the evidence immediately and took off! What a cat!

On the long walk home, Gloria asked, "What did you do with that fish head?"

I answered truthfully, "God's house cat ate it."

"Barbara," she pointed out, "there are no cats in Bangladesh. You could not have given that fish head to a Bengali cat!"

"I didn't feed it to a Bengali cat, Gloria. He was God's house cat."

I'm not sure to this day that my friend Gloria Thurman believes that God sent His house cat to rescue me. I admit it was beyond belief. But it was not beyond the God I followed to Bangladesh, that I follow today. He can do anything.

The rest of the rice and curry with assorted fish heads did not worry me. God always had a way. A few days later, I accompanied Tom and Gloria to a graduation dinner for over 20 young men who had completed TEE—Theological Education by Extension.

My bowl of rice and curry sauce arrived with a spectacular fish head on top. I said to Tom, "I don't deserve this fine tribute. What student made the top grade on his examination?"

A jubilant young man waved his hand wildly toward Tom. I exchanged bowls with the valedictorian.

Thank You, Lord!

THERE'S A HAIR IN MY CHICHARON

When I think of the thousands of missionaries who have eaten all manner of unusual, unfamiliar "goodies" for years, my few experiences pale in comparison.

For instance, Regina Howell, program director of Alabama WMU's WorldSong camp, was a missionary journeyman in Guatemala from 1991 through 1993. She had some "hairy" experiences.

Regina, a small-town girl from Alabama, knew God was leading her to Guatemala. She also knew that the menu in that Middle American country would not be peas and corn bread. She had already found some Alabama foods she did not care for. As a little girl, she had been fed turnip greens. Gross!

She would, at her mother's insistence, put a little dab of the despised greens on her fork and try to get it down. She would end up gagging and generally make mealtime at the Howells' a delight!

Off to Guatemala she went. After only two weeks in the country, she went to a little church in Cantel. Fortunately, she accompanied veteran missionaries George and Helen Hardeman.

When they arrived, women were standing around the cooking area with smoke billowing everywhere. George Hardeman remarked, "I guess they're going to feed us after the service."

"Horror struck me," Regina remembers. It was anything but clean. In addition, there was a cholera scare!

After the service, Regina was praying, "OK, God, I'll eat whatever they bring me, but help me not to die."

They brought around a plate with four "things" on it. Regina reached to pick up one, and then she realized all four were for her! Gingerly, she looked at the four unidentified objects. They were wrapped in cornhusks. They reminded her of Mexican *tamales*. But she had never seen anything like it in Hartselle, Alabama.

The "thing" was a *combrai*. It looked like mush in a cornhusk to Regina. She had no idea how to eat the *combrai*, so she watched the Hardemans. They peeled off the husks and began to eat. Regina did the same.

She says, "It wasn't so bad; it wasn't so good either, but I could eat it without gagging."

After being in Guatemala for a year and a half, Regina was an old hand. She had had many experiences out of her comfort zone.

She had a friend, Coni, a 25-year-old young mother. Coni came by to ask if Regina would go with her to buy some meat from a family that had killed a pig. That family had two sons, Miguel and Rigo, who were in Regina's Sunday School class.

After Coni finished her buying, she and the boys' mother started talking about *chicharon*. They asked if Regina had ever had *chicharon*. She admitted that she had not. From their descriptions, she believed they were saying "pork skins." In her mind she pictured little bags she had seen in the grocery store. She had never tasted any, but they looked pretty harmless.

She followed the women to the backyard where a crowd of people was watching a big black pot that was sitting over a fire. The pot was full of grease and the people were stirring whatever was in the pot with a big stick.

They pulled out a floating *chicharon*—a big pork skin—and served it to Regina. It had about an inch of fat that looked like clear shortening on the skin. It didn't look very appetizing, but she figured it would be tasteless. She picked it up and discovered—to her horror—big, long hairs sticking out of the skin!

Beyond a doubt, when her tongue touched even one of those hairs, she would gag—or even worse!

Regina prayed fervently, "Help me, Lord!" And the Lord gave her an idea. She sank her teeth into the inch of fat on the bottom of the skin and slid some of the fat into her mouth. She carefully avoided the hairy skin. After a few bites of the fat, the onlookers were satisfied and turned their attention back to the bubbling pot.

Thank You, Lord!

The Lord blessed Regina's willingness in this experience. Miguel and Rigo continued to come to her Sunday School class. Soon after, Miguel wanted to know how to accept Jesus as his Savior. It was Regina's first time to lead someone to the Lord in Spanish, but Miguel seemed to understand what he was doing and wanted to pray in his own words.

"Tears welled up in my eyes," Regina remembers. "I heard the sweetest prayer I've ever heard prayed, as he asked Jesus to forgive him of his sins, and come into his life."

Regina saw Miguel's baptism before her journeyman days were over. She invited his parents to come
to the baptism and they did.

Not long after Regina returned to the US, word
came that Miguel's parents had also accepted the
Lord and were faithfully attending church.

Regina rejoices that God used her "hairy" experience to glorify His name!

God can use even a *chicharon*! That's beyond belief!

GIVE THE LORD A FEW FISH AND LOAVES . . .

Maybe because I like to eat so much, the miracles
about food really stand out in the Scriptures for me.
The manna and quail in the desert wanderings, Elijah being fed by the ravens, Elijah and the widow of
Zarephath's oil and meal, and Jesus turning the water
into wine are but a few examples. However, my very
favorite is the spectacular miracle of the loaves and
the fish.

The feeding of the 5,000 is the only miracle that is
included in all four Gospels. Perhaps this is because it
illustrates so comprehensively that Jesus is concerned
about human need and is equal to the challenge.

Matthew's telling of the miracle is compelling: "As
evening approached, the disciples came to him and
said, 'This is a remote place, and it's already getting late.
Send the crowds away, so they can go to the villages
and buy themselves some food'" (Matt. 14:15 NIV).

Jesus answered the disciples simply: "You give
them something to eat."

It was as if Jesus was saying, "You did bring your
big picnic basket, didn't you?" Or, "Did you forget
the chuck wagon?" The disciples were quick to
answer, "We have here only five loaves of bread and
two fish"—one boy's lunch.

No doubt the disciples were staggered to look into the faces of those 5,000 men, plus women and children, and then look at the one little lunch basket that was found!

But the disciples brought what was available to the Master, and He blessed it. We should do the same. Our little bit with God is more than a great quantity without Him.

In the hands of Jesus the five loaves and two fish became more than enough to feed the multitude. Not only did they eat, they were satisfied. Not only did they eat, but 12 baskets of food were left over!

That is beyond belief!

EATING—A LOT—AND BEING SATISFIED IN TAIWAN

Rob and Nan Sugg have been Southern Baptist missionaries in Taiwan since 1977. They took their three young children, Harriet, Robert, and Carroll, to Taiwan with them. All through the years, the whole family has eaten a lot of wonderful Chinese food and they have been satisfied. They have, however, tried to avoid whole frogs, sea slugs, and raw fish!

Nearly 20 years after going to Taiwan, Rob and Nan had an amazing experience with food, and it also included an unbelievable "grace gift" from the Lord.

Rob was pastor of Living Water Church at that time. He felt that God wanted the church to have a time of prayer and fasting. He even knew the time frame: 40 days.

Fasting was not unknown to the church. They had fasted for special events and needs for some time. But the previous fasts had been for only a week, and people had signed up for certain meals to fast and pray. It was a good way to focus the whole church on a particular need and to see God at work.

This time Rob suggested that each person pray and determine what kind of fast God wanted each individual to do. He pointed out several choices: fast one meal a day, fast from one particular food, or fast one day a week. As the Suggs prayed about how God wanted them to fast, they felt they should fast for the whole 40 days. They began on January 16, 1996. They drank lots of water and drank juice and sports drinks to keep up their strength, but did not eat solid food.

Toward the end of January, a young American in Taiwan, David Moody, asked Rob if he would perform the wedding ceremony for himself and his girlfriend, Alisha Lin. Rob agreed to do so. Then David asked if the Suggs would go with him to the engagement proceedings and dinner and fill in as sort of substitute parents. None of David's family was in Taiwan, and the Suggs felt this was an opportunity to have a significant ministry in the life of this young couple. They told David they would be happy to stand in for his parents.

Alisha's family is Hakka, a distinctive people group that has very few Christians. Alisha was a believer, but her family was not. The Suggs knew that eating would be an important part of the celebration, and that their host would be terribly offended if they did not eat.

The Suggs were fasting!

They prayed about it. They realized that God had known about the engagement and wedding when He led them to fast. Rob felt that God would give them a grace gift. He felt they should go ahead to the engagement ceremony and go ahead and eat the meal.

The day of the engagement ceremony and meal was Day 24 of the Suggs' fast. Everything they knew or had read about fasting led them to believe they could be in big trouble if they ate a big meal after so mant days without solid food. But the more they prayed, the more certain they were that God would give them a grace gift.

The big day arrived. They drove to the mountain village of Meinong. The engagement ceremony took place in Alisha's family home, a quaint, old-fashioned Chinese farm house. Then it was time for the feast. Rob admits, "I prayed that I would not get sick and throw up on the table!"

The dishes started coming. First came the traditional cold platter: squid, baby octopi, raw fish, and *cashew nuts*! They both ate a few nuts. Course two was a lobster, something they love. They ate a good bit of lobster. The courses kept coming--roast goat ribs, shrimp and pineapple, beef and bamboo shoots, and much more. All of it was delicious.

The Suggs had agreed they would eat small amounts and they tried, but it was all too good to resist. So they ate a lot! At one point Nan said, "You would think we hadn't eaten in a month!"

Amazingly, the Suggs did not get sick. God had indeed given them a grace gift. The Suggs ate and ate and ate and enjoyed it all, and they were satisfied.

They returned to their fast the next day with no ill effects, just a wonderful memory of God's grace gift.

Any who have ever fasted would say emphatically, that is beyond belief!

3

And the Fire Wouldn't Burn

*I*n the 1960s an explosion occurred in a steam plant near Columbiana, Alabama. An employee in the plant, Wayne Stephens, was rushed to the burn unit at a hospital in Birmingham.

His wife, Toni, was a member of our caring Sunday School class. We purposed to help her in every way we could.

We prayed fervently for Wayne. We took care of their two children. We set up an around-the-clock schedule for one of us to be with Toni at the hospital at all times. Men from the steam plant kept vigil at the hospital as well. During that time each of us saw the horror of out-of-control fire, up close and personal.

During the precious moments of visitation, Toni would grab me, and the two of us were gowned and masked and led into Wayne's sterile room. It was a nightmare. There was no semblance of the handsome man I knew. And the smell of death filled the room. I could only hold Toni up and pray with all my heart.

Those days before Wayne died taught me to hate the devastation of fire.

With awe I share with you several stories of the hand of God. He has all dominion—even over the flames! Be prepared. It's beyond belief!

34

BEYOND BELIEF IN KADUNA, NIGERIA

Nigeria, the most populous country in Africa with over 130 million people, is also the most Baptist. More than 3.5 million belong to the Nigerian Baptist Convention.

It all began on August 5, 1850, when Southern Baptist missionary Thomas Jefferson Bowen took his first step on Nigerian soil.

Now, more than 150 years later, the Nigerian Baptist Convention claims more than 7,000 churches, stretching the length and breadth of that great nation. Baptist schools have trained thousands of children, young men, and women. In fact, the president of Nigeria, Olusegun Obasanjo, attended a Baptist boys' high school where he was introduced to Jesus Christ.

President Obasanjo is today a strong, dedicated Baptist. During the 150th anniversary celebration of the Nigerian Baptist Convention in April 2000, he was the star attraction. When he came to the podium in the filled stadium in Abeokuta, Nigeria, he was greeted enthusiastically as he led the crowd in singing "To God Be the Glory."

"This is one of the most fulfilling hours of my life," he said. "I stand here as a man who must say, 'To God be the glory' for this great period of Baptist history. May God grant to us more fruitful years of service."

One major obstacle to continued growth in Nigeria is Muslim-Christian unrest. Stretching across the top of Africa is a line of countries that are Muslim. They have moved steadily southward with any and all means at their disposal.

A news release from Kaduna, a town in predominantly Muslim northern Nigeria, points out that northern Nigeria has suffered many years of Muslim-Christian conflict. Clashes between rival Muslim groups, as well as attacks on Christians, have resulted in rioting and bloodshed. Militant Islamic groups—some reportedly directed by radical Muslim nations—have brought tensions to the boiling point. It is difficult for us to understand the mix in northern Nigeria. For instance, Izalah is a Muslim group intent on purifying Islam of innovations. Then add to that Jamatul Nasir Islam, a political council of Muslim *emirs*, *imams*, and scholars. This mix becomes even more dangerous with groups like the Maitasine, whose rites reportedly include drinking their enemies' blood.

In spite of this volatile opposition, Christianity continues to grow—even thrive. All of this in spite of the fact that since the 1980s, thousands of people—mostly Christians—have been killed in riots.

But God has intervened to protect His people on many occasions. One such occasion was in May 1992 in Kaduna.

Bob and Martha Hall, longtime Southern Baptist missionaries to Nigeria, were in Kaduna at the seminary. Martha shares the terror and some of the miracles of that May.

Martha recalls that it was graduation week at the seminary. On Sunday the seniors marched in caps and gowns to Bethel Baptist Church behind the compound for the baccalaureate service. When they returned to the seminary, they learned that Muslims had burned churches in town and were marching toward the school.

By Monday evening the mob had arrived crying, "Burn! Burn!" Martha says that rumblings were heard over the murderous cries. Thunder! This rumbling of thunder came soon after a telephone call came from a pastor in Texas on a telephone that had not worked for six months. The pastor called the Halls' daughter in the US, and they both started prayer chains. Amazingly, a tropical storm hit and drenched everything and everybody. And the fire wouldn't burn!

The mob fled, but returned on the second night. Again the thunder rolled in and torrential rains fell. Nothing would burn!

On the third night, a military bus was parked outside the compound, suggesting the presence of many soldiers. The seminary dodged disaster again. By the next day, many soldiers were evident and the military governor had called for peace.

Another unbelievable story emerged from the mayhem of that May. This one came from Nasara Baptist Church. They had suffered grievous losses. Their church had been burned. The pastor had been burned in his car. The arm of the associate pastor had been hacked off at the elbow as he helped people to escape.

The following Sunday, a group of the seminary teachers went to express their love and concern. They found the congregation praising the Lord! A deacon was preaching that the riot was their fault because they had not taught the Muslims of God's love. They were obligated to forgive them and to share the Lord with them.

From behind a tree, a Muslim young man came forward. "Tell me more about this religion of forgiveness," he asked. He confessed that he had been one of those who had burned their church. He had been sent to discover when the members of Nasara would be coming to burn their nearby mosque. It was difficult for the young man to understand forgiveness. He had been taught retaliation.

Another incredible story took place at Oore-ofe Baptist Church in March 1987. Despite threats from Muslim leaders, the congregation was gathered to worship. However, the Christians ran for their lives when they heard, "There is no God but Allah, and Muhammad is his prophet!" A gang of 200 was bearing down on the church with torches and cans of gasoline, screaming, "Burn down their church!"

Within minutes, the pastor, Fola Lateju, stood alone in the church. He decided to face the mob. He walked to the gate.

"What you are about to do is against the will of God," he said. "You will incur His wrath. Go back and tell those who sent you that this is against God's will."

Pastor Lateju asked the mob if they would burn a *Gidan Addu'a*—a house of prayer—which is what they call a mosque.

The leaders were upset and talked among themselves. Then they seized the pastor, poured gasoline over him, and set fire to his clothing.

And the fire didn't burn!

Amazing!

The mob wheeled around to a clump of grass and doused it with gasoline. They put a torch to the grass and it exploded into flames.

Again the mob charged Lateju, and again they drenched him in gasoline. A second time they attempted to torch him.

And again, the fire wouldn't burn!

Unbelievable!

With shaking hands, they again poured their gasoline on the young pastor and held their flaming torches all over him.

The fire refused to burn.

Beyond belief!

In anger, one of the attackers struck Pastor Lateju on the head with a machete. When he fell, bleeding and unconscious, they left him to die and marched on to another church. The church family came out and carried him to a hospital, where he was treated and soon recovered.

After receiving training in England on evangelism among Muslims, Pastor Fola Lateju served as a teacher at the Baptist seminary in Ogbomosho, Nigeria. He is now Dr. Fola Lateju, director of Missionary Organizations Department of the Nigerian Baptist Convention. He hates vengeance and violence. He refuses to fight fire with fire. He responds with love and mercy.

That, too, is beyond belief!

GOD AND THE FIERY FURNACE

Even as we read how God delivered Fola Lateju from the blazing torches of the angry mob in Nigeria, our minds flash back to a well-known Bible story. Shadrach, Meshach, and Abednego encountered a trial by fire and discovered that God is more powerful than any fiery furnace.

Their story is found in the Bible in Daniel. The first chapter of Daniel places the time of the events as the third year of the reign of Jehoiakim, king of Judah. This was around the sixth century B.C.

Nebuchadnezzar was the mighty king of Babylon. History records that Babylon's power was at its peak. They had defeated their strong enemies: Assyria and Egypt. Nebuchadnezzar then turned his attention to Palestine. The city of Jerusalem was captured, the Temple stripped, and the first group of exiles were taken to Babylon. Those first exiles apparently were the best in the country—"the most cultured, intelligent, and religious."

Jeremiah called those first exiles "good figs" (Jer. 24:5). Daniel describes them as youths with "no defect, who were good-looking, showing intelligence in every branch of wisdom, endowed with understanding, and discerning knowledge, and who had ability for serving in the king's court" (Dan. 1:4 NASB). Daniel 1:6–7 identifies four of these exceptional young men: Daniel, Shadrach, Meshach, and Abednego. The cream of the crop of the exiles were educated for three years in Babylon. Nebuchadnezzar wanted their Babylon-trained minds as well as their bodies. And Daniel, Shadrach, Meshach, and Abednego were master students. In fact, the four were ten times better than all the rest of the students.

In addition, Daniel had understanding of visions and dreams. This put the four in good stead when Nebuchadnezzar had a dream he could not interpret. God revealed the dream and its meaning to Daniel, and he explained it to the king.

The king was so pleased that he made Daniel ruler over the entire province of Babylon! Daniel asked that his three friends be named as administrators of Babylon. Nebuchadnezzar granted his request.

In the third chapter of Daniel, after Daniel had interpreted the king's dream, the king set to work making a huge image like the one in his dream. The statue was 90 feet high. It was built on the plain of Dura.

Then the king called everybody who was anybody to the dedication of the image. They were instructed that when they heard the sound of the horn, flute, lyre, and other instruments, they were to fall down and worship the golden image.

The people were warned of the consequences of refusing to worship. They would be cast into a furnace of blazing fire.

Steven R. Miller, in his commentary, explains that a huge kiln had been built to smelt metal for the idol that had been constructed.[1] The temperature in the kiln could reach 1,800°F![2]

Therefore, when Nebuchadnezzar's band began to play, the people fell to the ground as they had been commanded to do.

Except for three: Shadrach, Meshach, and Abednego.

Almost immediately, certain Babylonians seized upon their refusal as the perfect opportunity to rid themselves of the foreign intruders. They approached the king and reminded him that he was to throw into the furnace those who failed to worship the image. Then they jubilantly crowed, "Those Jews didn't bow!"

King Nebuchadnezzar was furious! He called the three offenders and asked if the charge was true.

It was true.

The king offered another chance. The royal orchestra would play again.

They refused. "Our God may save us," they answered, but they made it clear that even if God did not save them, they still would not worship the image of gold or the king's gods.

Shadrach, Meshach, and Abednego had accepted the fact that God does not always choose to intervene miraculously in human circumstances, even on behalf of his servants. Miller paints a valuable lesson for believers today: "Does God have all power? Yes. Is God able to deliver believers from all problems and trials? Yes. But does God deliver believers from all trials? No. . . . The purpose . . . may not always be understood, but God simply asks that His children trust Him—even when it's not easy."[3]

At this point, it was not easy for the three Hebrews. The king lost it! He ordered the furnace heated seven times hotter than usual!

Nebuchadnezzar commanded some of his strongest soldiers to tie the three up and throw them into the flames. The fire was so fierce that the soldiers were killed as they cast them in.

The king went to the furnace and had a heart-stopping discovery: four men were in the furnace. And they were walking around, unbound, unharmed!

Nebuchadnezzar himself said, "The fourth looks like a son of the gods" (Dan. 3:25 NIV).

The king called, "Shadrach, Meshach, and Abednego, servants of the Most High God, come out! Come here!" (Dan. 3:26).

They came out! They probably danced out! By this time there was a crowd. They crowded around. They saw that their bodies had not been burned, not a hair on their heads had been singed, their robes were not scorched. They didn't even smell smoky!

This story is beyond belief!

THE FIRE MAY BURN, BUT IT WILL NOT DESTROY THE SPIRIT

The conflicts in Nigeria continue, as this incredible story will show.

The first frantic email out of Kaduna, Nigeria, was at 11:15 A.M. Nigerian time on February 22, 2000. Southern Baptist missionary Ray Davidson alerted stateside missionaries and retired missionaries of the burning of the Baptist seminary in Kaduna.

Ray Davidson began by saying, "I write this with a very heavy heart." Then he shared news of the horrible attack. Less than an hour earlier, he had talked with a seminary student on campus while the invasion was taking place. The attackers were approaching the president's office from the library, and the student had to run for his life.

At 10:00 A.M., the United States embassy had advised missionaries Dale and Brenda Gray to attempt to get to the Nigerian Air Force base about one mile north of the seminary for safety. They fled from the back of the campus over an eight-foot-high wall, along with the wives and children of the faculty and students.

At about the same time, the mob had breached the eastern wall of the compound. They had made their way through the compound, looting, destroying, and burning the classrooms, chapel, and administration building. The faculty and students had attempted to defend the campus but were slowly pushed back. Their defense allowed their wives and children to escape with no injuries from the attackers.

Ray Davidson added on this first email that the day before the seminary attack, 11 churches in Kaduna had been burned. Four of them were Baptist. Radio reports numbered 20 casualties.

The following day, February 23, 2000, Ray wrote his second email. First, he thanked his readers for their prayers. Then he relayed a report from Dale Gray, who had been to the seminary that morning.

The good news: According to student pastors, most, if not all, of the students and their families were safe. No deaths had been reported. Most students and their families, as well as many of the faculty families, were safe at the Air Force base. Nearly 1,000 refugees were at that place, though not all of them were connected with the seminary. Already Dale, his wife, Brenda, and others were providing food and other help. By the end of the week, refugees were numbering about 5,000.

Then the bad news: There were casualties, but their identities were still unknown.

The buildings on the campus were in ruins. All of the classrooms, the chapel, and the administration buildings had been destroyed. Student dormitories had been heavily damaged. Roofs remained, but there was extensive fire damage. All of the library books were gone, as was the library itself. (The seminary had just reached the goal of 10,000 books that was required for accreditation.) Dale also reported that First Baptist Church across the street and the Seminary Annex were gone.

The nursing office and three faculty houses were looted but not burned. The president's home and two missionary houses were left intact, as security forces had arrived before the mob reached them.

Ray Davidson ended his second email by requesting prayer for the seminary leaders, especially the seminary's president, Uche Enyioha, and his wife, Oche.

Again, later on the 23rd, Ray sent a third email, updating the Kaduna situation. It was confirmed that two seminary family members and the school driver's 16-year-old son had been killed.

On Thursday after the attack, Ray sent another email. At this point he had talked with Dr. Enyioha, the seminary's president, about the attack. Dr. Enyioha related that when he saw the seminary surrounded by the mob, he prayed that a massacre would not take place. The campus had 295 students plus children, faculty members, and families, in addition to some others who had taken refuge at the school.

Dr. Enyioha said that the forces of darkness were at the gates of the seminary with no help in sight. There seemed to be no avenue for escape.

Ray then shared with Dr. Enyioha that he had been getting the word out from his house in Abuja, the capital of Nigeria, and that people around the world had been praying even as the attack was taking place.

Dr. Enyioha assured Ray that those prayers had been answered, for God made a way of escape for over 400 people on the campus. Sadly, five had been killed and others had been injured. One of those killed was Deacon Bako, a recently retired seminary maintenance man. However, most of the faculty, students, and their families had made it to safety. Their escapes were miraculous—beyond belief!

And the Lord was not through. When Dale and Brenda Gray fled, 21-year-old Daniel Bako led them through the bush. If Daniel had been home with his father, Deacon Bako, he surely would have been killed, as his father was. After Daniel led the Grays to safety, he started home. He saw the attackers and quickly hid in a ditch under some rubbish. The attackers walked directly over him without discovering their prey!

A third miracle was the miracle of the telephones. Both telephones at the seminary had only been working on and off for several months before the attack. They worked perfectly the day of the attack, as well as the following day!

The second part of the telephone miracle concerned Ray Davidson's telephone in Abuju. His phone was working clearly and he was able to successfully pass information between Kaduna, the Nigerian Baptist Convention office in Ibadan, and the United States embassy, as well as missionaries and families in the US. Many prayer warriors went to the Lord on Kaduna's behalf.

Nigerian president Olusegun Obasanjo, in a nationwide broadcast after two weeks of bloody clashes—during which the seminary was burned—called for reconciliation between Muslims and Christians. Sources reported more than 1,000 deaths. Thousands were left homeless, and at least 36 churches were destroyed, as well as several mosques.

President Obasanjo said, "What I saw was disheartening and upsetting. The devastation was so massive. It seemed as though Kaduna had overnight been turned into a battlefield."

After the smoke was gone, Baptists in Nigeria sifted through the ashes and attempted to count the cost. The final count at the seminary was five seminary family members killed, including Deacon Bako, three student pastors, and the son of the school bus driver. Several other people had been killed near the campus. The cost of replacing the destroyed buildings on campus will be several million dollars, not including replacing furnishings, personal belongings, and library books. However, Nigerian Baptists say that the destruction, even the loss of life, will not stop the growth of God's kingdom in Nigeria.

Emeritus missionary Payton Myers, the former principal of the seminary at Kaduna, traveled to Nigeria to help repair a men's dormitory on campus, arriving just as the attack was beginning. After the violence subsided, Payton took corn, cassava, and other food to the air force base where both Muslims and Christians had taken refuge.

Payton declares that despite the physical damage to buildings and the loss of life, the attacks in Kaduna are no setback for the churches there.

"The church, the kingdom of God, is not in buildings made with human hands, but in the hearts of those who have been touched by God," says Payton. "The burning of buildings will never stop the movement of the church in Nigeria or anywhere else. From the ashes will come a strong, more alive church."

That is the stuff of miracles, and it is beyond belief!

---

[1] Stephen R. Miller, *The New American Commentary*, vol. 18, *Daniel* (Nashville: Broadman & Holman Publishers, 1994), 115, quoting G. L. Archer, Jr., "Daniel," EBC (Grand Rapids: Zondervan, 1985), 56.
[2] Stephen R. Miller, *The New American Commentary*, vol. 18, *Daniel* (Nashville: Broadman & Holman Publishers, 1994), 115.
[3] Ibid., 120.

4

Somebody Loves Me

*B*anners lined the roadway from a small Kurdish village. The body of Chickie Hood was on its way home to Alabama. The taxi she and another volunteer had been riding in had collided with a minibus, and she had been killed.

It was 1992. Chickie, a Southern Baptist, had been serving as a relief worker among Kurdish refugees in northern Iraq for nearly a year. During those months, Chickie Hood had made a tremendous impression on the Kurds. She had left her job as a nurse at University Hospital in Birmingham, Alabama, to work with Global Partners, a London-based relief and development agency. She had helped operate mobile medical clinics. The Kurds saw her as one working as a doctor, diagnosing and treating their illnesses. Their tributes on those farewell banners were eloquent and heartfelt:

DR. CHICKIE HOOD: MARTYR OF KURDISTAN

DR. CHICKIE HOOD: FRIEND OF THE KURDS

Global Partners had been involved in efforts to aid the Kurds since the end of the Persian Gulf War in 1991. The Kurds had revolted against Saddam Hussein's regime. His bloodthirsty reprisal drove thousands of Kurds from their homes into the mountains. A stunned world watched Saddam's obliteration as he reduced Kurd villages to rubble.

More than a million Kurds fled to Iraq's borders with Turkey and Iran, awaiting help. Hundreds died daily due to cold, exposure, disease, and starvation.

The Foreign Mission Board (now called International Mission Board) geared up to respond to the crisis. Tim Brendle was asked to lead the Board's Gulf War Response Unit. Joining Global Partners and more than 20 other agencies, organizations, and military units, Southern Baptists embarked upon a huge relief effort.

The Kurds may have been unknown to the world at that time, but they were known to the Foreign Mission Board. They had been one of the first groups highlighted in the Board's prayer efforts for unreached people in the world.

WHO ARE THE KURDS?

Kurds are an ethnic group with a population greater than 15 million (maybe even 20 million), yet they are without a country. They are displaced people. Most Kurds live in southern Turkey, Iran, Iraq, and Syria. However, Kurds also have migrated to Russia, Kuwait, Lebanon, and western Europe. Approximately 4,000 live in the United States.

The majority of the Kurds live in the Persian Gulf region. Since the thirteenth century the region has been called Kurdistan. The region covers the area where the borders of Iran, Iraq, Turkey, and Syria meet. The Zagros Mountains and much of the Tigris and Euphrates rivers are in Kurdistan.

WHERE DID THE KURDS COME FROM?

The Kurds have been around a long time—over 4,000 years! They are probably descendants of the Medes.

Darius, the Median king of Persia during Daniel's time (see Dan. 5:31) was an outstanding forefather, as was Saladin, one of the greatest champions of Islam at the time of the Crusades.

WHY DON'T THEY HAVE A HOMELAND OF THEIR OWN?

In writing his report called *The Kurds: A Nation Denied*, David McDowall addressed this question in the third chapter, called "Hidden from history—the Kurds before 1920."[1]

Throughout their history, the Kurds put tribal allegiance first. In fact, the first push for statehood did not come until 1880. It went nowhere.

Before World War I, the Kurds were split between the Ottoman and Persian empires. When the war ended, the Treaty of Sevres promised a unified, independent Kurdish homeland. The treaty was never ratified.

There followed a string of brutal acts and heartbreaking betrayals:

1925: In Turkey under Ataturk, the speaking of Kurdish languages was forbidden. All revolts were brutally suppressed.

1946: A Soviet-backed Kurdish republic was formed in Iran. The Soviets withdrew their support, and Iran marched in and took over.

1961: Armed Kurdish resistance began against Iraqi rule.

1970: After nearly ten years of fighting, Iraq promised political representation for the Kurds if they would enact a cease-fire. Iraq did not follow through.

1975: The Shah of Iran, with the support of others, aided rebelling Iraqi Kurds in an attempt to weaken Saddam. Later in 1975, Iran and Iraq made peace with each other. The Kurds were left without Iranian support and bit the dust again.

1980: Saddam began his "scorched earth" campaign against the Kurds during the Iran-Iraq War. He razed 5,000 Kurdish villages.

1988: Saddam launched a chemical attack on the town of Halabja, killing 5,000 Kurds. Hundreds of thousands fled to Turkey and Iran.

1991: After the Persian Gulf War, Saddam took out his rage on the Kurds. He killed thousands, forcing another Kurdish "run-for-your-life" for survival.

After the Kurds fled from their villages, Iran peppered the earth with landmines to "welcome" the Kurds back to their homes. They also used chemicals. They poisoned wells and water sources.

Is it any wonder that the Kurds felt they had no friends? Promises were made. Promises were broken. Alliances were made. Alliances were forsaken.

Is it any wonder that one book about the Kurds is entitled *No Friends But the Mountains: The Tragic History of the Kurds*?[2]

Paul Smith, director of Kurdish relief for Global Partners in the early 1990s, echoes this sentiment: "The Kurds often told us, 'Kurds have no friends!'"

In the November 1999 issue of *National Geographic*, assistant editor Mike Edwards reported on the suffering of the Kurds. He told of the modest measure of protection from the United States and British airplanes patrolling no-fly zones to keep Iraqi aircraft from flying there. However, killing still continued.

A priest in northern Iraq who was questioned by Edwards indicated that the people were numb. "They have lived with war for so many years they don't care. Nearly every family has lost someone. Life is very cheap here."[3]

And life will remain fragile. Consider the missiles that might still be fired. Consider the ever-present Kalashnikov rifles. Consider the millions of land

50

mines. It has been estimated that decades will pass before Kurdistan is cleared of mines, grenades, and unexploded mortar shells.

The plight of the Kurds is beyond belief! Doesn't anybody care? Doesn't anybody love them?

GOD DID A MIGHTY WORK

In a challenging report to the Foreign Mission Board in 1991, Tim Brendle put the facts before the Board:

"In the parching aftermath of the fiery, high-tech war in the gulf, God began His mighty work of moving one of the greatest unreached people groups of the world into the center of the global stage. Fighting incredible difficulties, the Kurdish people fled from the onslaught of the Iraqi army into northern Iraq, Turkey, and across the mountainous western border of Iran. They seemed to be the people whom the world had forgotten—the people who had no friends."

In light of the tremendous needs, an amazing response came from many different groups. President George Bush asked the US military and relief agencies to deliver blankets to the Kurds. Texas Baptist Men became involved and Southern Baptists sent over 34,000 blankets.

Mike Stroope, a Southern Baptist who worked with Global Partners, went to Turkey to see what needed to be done. Hunger and relief funds came immediately from the Foreign Mission Board. Mike also requested medical volunteers, translators, and logistics helpers.

Swedish Christians and other evangelicals partnered with the team. Close contact was maintained with all sorts of officials: Turkish, Kurdish, United Nations, and the US embassy. An outpatient dispensary began operation and ministered to hundreds of Kurds a day.

Iran had been closed to Americans and most of the Christian world for years. Yet—beyond belief—Iranian officials asked for help! It had to be God's doing!

Again a great coordination of effort took place. The first relief team was a Korean Baptist team from the Baptist hospital in Pusan, Korea. Close behind came US volunteers aboard a cargo plane full of portable kitchens, water purifiers, and medical supplies. The cargo plane was courtesy of LESEA Ministries, a charismatic group based in South Bend, Indiana.

Add to the mix the Red Crescent Society (the Middle Eastern equivalent of the Red Cross), and Norwegian and Finnish Lutheran volunteers. Iranian Christians were also deeply involved.

No longer were the Kurds forgotten.

By the middle of 1991, over 60 volunteers had participated in relief efforts to the Kurds. They included nonresidential and residential missionaries, International Service Corps personnel, and short-term volunteers. Many agencies, organizations, and military units had been partners. Nine nationalities had worked together. Eight additional nationalities had given aid indirectly.

Tim Brendle remarked, "We are one body with many members, and truly we have demonstrated that we have one Lord."

LOVING THE KURDS

Those who responded to the horrendous needs of the Kurds will never forget their experiences or the people. They became prayer warriors for the Kurds. The walls of isolation, the walls of indifference, even the walls of Islam had been breached.

One of those involved at the crisis point at the end of the Gulf War was Southern Baptist nurse Donna Rye, who had been serving in Mexico. She was asked to serve on a medical team in Iraq.

"Tent cities" had been set up for the refugees. There were three camps with approximately 20,000 Kurds in each camp. Each of the three camps had medical services and a temporary hospital. Donna served in the second camp, working with personnel from many different countries, including some doctors from the military and other relief organizations.

Donna worked in the tent for women and children's each day from early morning to late afternoon. They saw from 100 to 300 patients almost every day for a full month.

When the Kurds had escaped to the mountains, it was winter and bitterly cold. There was much snow. Donna recalls seeing patients with malaria, typhoid, land mine wounds, gunshot wounds, intestinal worms, scabies, lice, and lots of burns from cooking on open fires.

Donna says there are "thousands of stories." One day she had washed a toddler with a solution to take care of scabies. The solution produced an allergic effect, and the child began screaming.

"I took water to wash the solution off, but it took some time and she was screaming at the top of her lungs," Donna remembers. "So I began to hum to her 'Jesus Loves Me' and almost immediately she calmed down. I think of that in the context of the calming effect that the name of Jesus can have in all of our lives. The power of the very name."

Donna recalls another wonderful memory involving a young couple from Europe who joined their group. The couple walked throughout the grounds of the camp and prayed for the salvation of the Kurds.

Donna had not heard of the concept of prayerwalking at that time, and was impressed by their sincerity.

Donna finished her month's work and returned to Mexico. Then she returned to Iraq a second time. By that time the Kurds in the camps had been resettled in their villages. Global Partners was in the business of conducting mobile clinics and drilling wells.

Donna went out with the mobile clinics. They saw patients in a different village each day, seven days a week. Sometimes they had volunteer doctors. Sometimes it was a nurse-only clinic.

As if enough hadn't happened, the Turks accused the Kurds of raiding their villages. They retaliated by bombing some of the Kurdish villages.

The week before Donna arrived, a Kurdish village was bombed just before a medical team arrived. Some of the Kurds had been killed, and others were badly wounded. The team patched up the wounded and took them to the nearest hospital. The hospital had been destroyed by Saddam. It had very poor equipment and blood was spattered everywhere. Used needles were all over the floor. "It was almost as dangerous being in the hospital as being at home," Donna remembers.

Paul Smith and his wife, Virginia, went to northern Iraq in 1991 to relieve Mike Stroope for two months. They ended up staying until the end of 1995.

Paul describes the working conditions of the volunteers who came to aid the Kurds: "We worked . . . sometimes seeing 500 patients a day . . . in tents where the temperature sometimes reached 130°F in the heat of summer."

Paul adds that the volunteers lived in a house with primitive toilet facilities. Virginia Smith cooked for the volunteers. This was quite a challenge since there was often little food in the market.

Because of the intense heat, most slept on cots on the roof. Sometimes as many as 18 volunteers crowded the roof. "One night one of the staff came up to the roof late and was preparing to lie down on his cot, only to hear the scream of a nurse who had taken his cot by mistake," laughs Paul.

Some laughter helped them deal with all the hard realities. Paul told of the many malnourished babies they treated. He says, "When you see a child die in your arms because he or she had no food or milk for days, it causes you to want to open a facility to help them."

So a Well Baby Clinic was opened. Over 500 babies were saved by giving them whole milk powder and high-protein biscuits.

The medical staff determined that impure water was infecting over half the people. The wells had been destroyed and the toilet habits of the people caused pollution of the streams. Therefore, the volunteers drilled wells and constructed spring boxes. A spring box is a sealed concrete box built over a spring with a pipe leading down to a village, where one faucet is placed for every five families. Over 200 deep-water wells were drilled and over 40 spring-box systems were built.

When the Kurds returned to their villages, they had nothing but the clothes on their backs. The United Nations gave each family a piece of plastic to use in making a lean-to shelter. Then the families would make mud bricks and build a house to better protect themselves from the snow and bitter cold. That's right—130°F in the summer and bitterly cold in the winter!

The Kurds had no tools, no food. Some agencies gave them flour, sugar, tea, and other foodstuff. Global Partners decided to give them seeds. Five kinds of vegetable seeds (chosen by the Kurds) were given to over 6,000 families. Paul tells of seeing all the members of some of these families, aged four and up, digging with sticks to plant the seeds to keep from starving.

Later, 8,000 families received rice and wheat seeds to plant. A Kurdish friend who was an engineer suggested that the team help rebuild the old water-powered mills. Saddam had destroyed the buildings, but the stone-grinding wheels were intact. Cement and a little iron were furnished, and the Kurds themselves rebuilt the mills. About 400,000 Kurds were then able to have flour and processed rice.

INCREASED DANGER

The help being given to the Kurds was despised by Saddam. Unbelievably, he offered $10,000 to any Kurd who would shoot or blow up a foreigner. It was inevitable that the team became targets.

On one occasion, a medical team was ambushed on the way to conduct a mobile clinic. Dr. Robert Pepper miraculously dodged a bullet. The Kurdish driver pulled over and everyone ran for cover. One Kurd said to a tall doctor, "Keep your head down!"

"I'm running with my head between my knees now!" retorted the doctor.

Another incident involved one of the well-drilling teams. They were ambushed and two rocket-propelled grenades were fired at the vehicles. Paul notes that carrying defensive weapons is not normal missions policy, but it became their policy in order to stay in Iraq.

The lives of the volunteers were touched and changed during this time. Cathy Dunn, one of the volunteer nurses, admits that it was for her "a time of dependence on the Lord" that invigorated her prayer life. She adds that she gained a personal conviction to pray for world leaders—including Saddam Hussein!

So What Has Happened to the Kurds?

Is it the same old story of death and betrayal for the Kurds?

It is for certain that many Kurds have died due to harsh treatment and reprisals. However, many Kurds now know beyond a doubt—*somebody loves me.*

In the early days of the Persian Gulf Response, Tim Brendle said, "The Kurds are a hidden people who have been locked out of the reach of the gospel of Jesus Christ by political and geographical boundaries. Christians need to become aware of their situation and pray earnestly that our Lord will open a way for the gospel to reach into their lives."

Was the Persian Gulf Response that opening?

Paul Smith says simply, "Our intent was to show them the love of Jesus by helping them in their deep distress. As our doctors and nurses treated them, they experienced that love."

Yes, somebody loves me!

A tribal chief told Paul after the wells and water spring boxes were finished: "All our lives we will tell our children and grandchildren how you Christians loved us and helped us!"

Yes, somebody loves me!

Buddy Kellett, a Southern Baptist volunteer well driller, was questioned by his Kurdish landlord about why he had come halfway around the world—without getting paid—to help the Kurds have clean water.

"You and I are brothers, although we might be half a world apart," Buddy replied. "When you hurt, I hurt."

Yes, somebody loves me!
Freshly cooked rice, enriched with lentils and raisins, fed 10,000 Kurds in Iran each day. *"Soo pas,"* Kurdish for *thank you,* echoed through the camp. A group of Iranian Christians, as well as scores of Kurdish refugees, helped clean the rice and raisins, operate the stoves, and clean the pots. There was unbridled joy!

A Kurdish immigrant to the United States who had accompanied the feeding team told the Kurds: "These people are here because of Jesus. He loves us."
Yes, somebody loves me!
"The Bible tells me so!"
The Kurds have never had the Scriptures in their own language. This became a real concern for the volunteers working in Iraq. A coalition of like-minded relief organizations was formed, translators and scholars were enlisted, and in less than two years, the Bible was translated and on computer. Four books of the New Testament were printed in Iraq and distributed. Since so few books were available in Kurdish, the district governor asked about its use in the schools.
Yes, somebody loves me!
"The Bible tells me so!"
A local *imam*, a Muslim religious leader, visited the feeding camp and blessed the operation. To the amazement of the team members, the *imam* blessed them, anointing their hands with rose oil. As the team left the camp, hundreds of Kurdish refugees lined the road for a mile to the camp entrance, cheering the feeding team! The Iranian troops then fired a military gun salute.

Tim Brendle says, "Truly our God was glorified."
Yes, somebody loves me!
In a letter to friends, Chickie Hood said, "The people are wonderful! Loving, kind, generous, and

humorous. They've suffered much and continue to endure. I've seen so many destroyed villages, treated wounds from hand grenades and land mines. Some families have had their homes destroyed seven times."

Yes, Chickie Hood loves me, and Paul Smith, and Tim Brendle, and hundreds of volunteers from all over the world!

Tim Brendle pronounced a benediction on this part of this book: "May this chapter . . . make [the Kurds] a little better known to the Baptist family and may God use us to love them so they can come to know His grace, love, and peace."

That is no longer beyond belief, for now many Kurds know:

Somebody loves me!

SOMEBODY LOVES THE SAMARITANS

Must there always be the Kurds? Or must there always be the _____? (You fill in the blank.)

Or the Samaritans?

It could be said that the Iranians, the Iraqis, and the Turks hate the Kurds in much the same way that the Jews hated the Samaritans in biblical times.

This hatred was deep-seated. Read 2 Kings, chapter 17. The Jews considered the Samaritans to be heathens. They were descendants of the people that Shalmaneser had brought in to repopulate desolated Israel after the exile.

The Samaritans were a mixed race. Some Jews were not taken into captivity in Babylon but were left to care for the land and the vineyards. As the years went on, these "left behind" Jews intermarried with people sent from Babylon. The children of such marriages were "not pure"—a very important matter to the Jews.

The mixing of the people also brought religious havoc. The Babylonians brought their own native styles of worship. In 2 Kings 17:41 we see the sorry state of worship: "So while these nations feared the Lord, they also served their idols."

In addition, the Samaritans' bible was a copy of the Law of Moses with text altered to suit them. The Jews considered the Samaritan religion a mutilated Judaism.

Hatred was intense. In every synagogue the Samaritans were cursed. This bitter enmity continued to the time of Christ when the Jews had "no dealings" with the Samaritans (see John 4:9).

Even though a direct route would cause Jews from Galilee to go to Jerusalem through Samaria, no Jew would do so. Galilean Jews would skirt Samaria and go by the way of Peraea.

Only God's love could overleap the boundaries of hatred. Consider the wonderful story of the Good Samaritan (Luke 10:25–35). Consider the woman at the well (John 4:1–42).

In Jesus' parable, the Good Samaritan was *good*. He was compassionate. His example was more to be admired than the Jewish religious leaders who passed by the injured man.

The woman at the well was not necessarily good, but she was made whole through the love of Christ. Jesus showed His love by talking with her.

God did not tell us to go and share the gospel with people we like or admire. He did not tell us to go to the responsive people. He commanded us to go to the ends of the earth—to all people everywhere.

He showed us He loved the Samaritans.

He shows us He loves the Kurds.

He loves those people you wrote on that blank line on page 58.

Somebody loves me!

God loves me!

May that love overflow in each of us, so that we can mean it when we say to a lost and dying world, "I love *you!*"

That is not beyond belief.

The Cross is beyond belief.

[1] David McDowall, *The Kurds: A Nation Denied* (London: Minority Rights Publications, 1992), 25–35.

[2] John Bulloch and Harvey Morris, *No Friends But the Mountains: The Tragic History of the Kurds* (New York: Oxford University Press, 1992).

[3] Mike Edwards, "Eyewitness Iraq," *National Geographic* 196, no. 5 (November 1999): 2–27.

5

Who's the Fairest One of All?

I always loved the part in "Snow White" when the wicked queen looked into her mirror and asked:
Mirror, mirror on the wall,
Who's the fairest one of all?
And the mirror answered back:
Snow White is the fairest one of all.
You know how the story goes, with the wicked queen plotting to do away with her competition, the beautiful Snow White.

It seems the "snow white" hearts still have a hard time. The world still plots against the beauties of today, but God's mirror reveals the wicked queen every time.

Let's shift our focus to a biblical beauty who had a pure heart and the courage of a godly queen.

A whole Old Testament book, Esther, tells her story. Michael Avi-Yonah, author of *Our Living Bible*, points out that the book is a "vividly told romance about the miraculous deliverance of the Jews from extermination in the days of the Persian Empire."[1]

The first character we meet in the book is King Ahasuerus (also called Xerxes). Ahasuerus is pictured in Greek sources as a temperamental monarch. In addition, he was much given to sensual pleasures. His style of governing was to delegate his royal duties to trusted ministers.

The plot thickens when King Ahasuerus throws a huge banquet. "In the third year of his reign, he gave a banquet for all his princes and attendants, the army officers of Persia and Media, the nobles, and the princes of his provinces being in his presence" (Esther 1:3 NASB).

The kingdom of Ahasuerus included 127 provinces and stretched from India to Ethiopia. When he held a banquet, it was lavish beyond belief. The first chapter of the book describes the seven-day (and night) event. Avi-Yonah suggests that "the guests reclined on sumptuous couches inlaid with gold and silver, in pavilions of white, green, and blue. The drink was served in vessels of gold" of different ornate shapes. "Many artistically wrought Persian gold vessels have survived the centuries. Perhaps some of these were used at the banquet of King Ahasuerus."[2]

The king had a reigning queen—Queen Vashti. She was giving her own party for women apart from the men. It was held in the palace away from the king's garden party.

On the seventh day of the banquet, King Ahasuerus commanded Vashti to come to his party. Perhaps his guests had tired of his musicians, his entertainment.

His command was unheard of. The royal consort stayed within the walls of the palace. Queen Vashti indignantly refused to "go on display." Perhaps Vashti should be the heroine of this story!

Vashti was granted an immediate Persian divorce—a banishment from the palace! A search committee was appointed and a long search was conducted to find the most beautiful virgin in the whole vast empire.

Many young women applied for the queenhood. They entered training at the palace to assure their selection as "the fairest one of all."

Because of her beauty, Esther was a definite candidate. Esther was a Jew. Her uncle and guardian was Mordecai, who advised her not to mention that she was Jewish.

For 12 months all the selected young women were beautified. They had 6 months with oil of myrrh and 6 months with spices and cosmetics. It was a Persian spa treatment!

Finally, the king called for Esther and she found favor with him. He set the royal crown on her head and made her his queen.

After Esther became queen, Mordecai exposed two of the king's chamberlains who were plotting against Ahasuerus. His good deed was recorded in the royal chronicle.

At this point, enter Haman. He quickly rose to prime minister and was all-powerful. He also had a burning hatred of Jews and especially Mordecai, who refused to bow to him.

Very cleverly, Haman devised a plan to exterminate the Jews and confiscate their property. He talked Ahasuerus into signing the decree.

Mordecai got word to Esther about Haman's evil plan. When Mordecai told Esther to intercede, she explained she couldn't go to the king unless he summoned her. Any person daring to go in on his or her own would be put to death unless the king held out his scepter.

Mordecai's reply to Esther is classic: "Do not imagine that you in the king's palace can escape any more than all the Jews. For if you remain silent at this time, relief and deliverance will arise for the Jews from another place and you and your father's house will perish. And who knows whether you have not attained royalty for such a time as this?" (Esther 4:13–14).

Esther made her decision. She asked Mordecai to gather all the Jews and ask them to fast for three days. She and her maidens would do the same. Then she'd go to the king. She said resolutely, "And if I perish, I perish" (Esther 4:16).

The king extended his scepter to Esther and asked her to come near. He asked her what she wanted and Esther invited him and Haman to a banquet—which led to a second banquet.

Haman was thrilled over the invitation. He just knew he was going to be given a great recognition. He would ask for the hanging of Mordecai. In fact, he had a gallows built for the hanging.

However, the night before the banquet, Ahasuerus read some of the chronicles and discovered how Mordecai had saved his life!

He called Haman in and asked how he could honor a really great man. Haman, believing himself to be the really great man, poured it on thick: a royal robe, one of the king's horses, a royal crown, and a royal reception with all honoring him.

All of this pleased the king, and he sent Haman to honor Mordecai. Haman was devastated!

Haman then went to the second banquet, where Esther revealed Haman's horrible plans. The king ordered Haman to be hung on the very gallows he had built for Mordecai. That is beyond belief!

To this day, fair Esther is honored by Jews all over the world.

WHO'S THE FAIREST OF THEM ALL IN PAKISTAN?

When I wrote *Not Simply with Words*, the biography of International Mission Board missionary, Susan Ingouf Lafferty, I met Ayeshah, another who is one of "the fairest of them all."

Actually I first met "A." For a year I prayed, as Susan directed in her letters, for a beautiful young woman named "A." I don't pray well for a letter of the alphabet, but as I prayed for Susan, somehow "A" slipped into my prayers.

Right after the New Year of 1994 rolled around, Todd Lafferty, pastor of the International Church of Karachi, performed the wedding ceremony of "A" and her fiancé. Susan attended the ceremony but didn't dream that "A" would become such a dear friend.

About the time of the wedding, Susan was having a rough time. In her journal she wrote some words from Psalm 86: "Give me a sign of Your goodness, that my enemies may see it and be put to shame" (Ps. 86:17). Then she lamented, "Sometimes that's what I long for in the wilderness years—just a sign of Your goodness that the enemies of doubt and dryness and busyness may see it and be put to shame!"

Less than two weeks later, Todd and Susan saw the newlyweds. They invited them to come visit the International Church of Karachi—and they came the following Sunday!

Three days later, Ayeshah asked Todd about women's Bible studies. The studies had been canceled for the summer, but Todd told her that Susan might do a study with her. Ayesha said she'd really like that!

Susan was elated! "Lord, is this the answer to my heartcry?"

Ayeshah and Susan started meeting every Monday evening to study the Gospel of John.

After the first meeting, Susan wrote: "Lord, I can't judge if Ayeshah is a Christian or not. Sounds like she's a believer—though still struggling with Who Christ is. . . . I shared the bridge illustration and she seemed to agree. When I asked if she'd made a decision like that, she said yes. . . . But she refers to it as 'converting to Christianity' instead of 'choosing to follow Christ.'"

At one point Susan said to Ayeshah, "You've probably heard this." She began quoting John 3:16. "For God so loved the world . . ." then stopped. "Have you?"

Ayeshah had never heard it. Susan quoted it all to her with tears in her eyes. "Lord, thank You for entrusting me with the privilege of giving her spiritual guidance. Give me *wisdom* in this. I pray You will teach her Who Jesus is, even this week."

The second study session included the question, "Have you ever 'received' Jesus as your Savior and Lord? If so, when?"

Susan shared her own experience of becoming a Christian.

Ayeshah answered that God had been speaking to her since childhood. Even in school she never prayed the written prayers; she had just prayed to God. She added, "I've received Him as Savior just since we began this study!"

Susan wrote in her journal, "Thank You, Lord! Thank You for Your work in Ayeshah's life. Thank You for her teachable heart, her desire to know You more and more!"

Later Susan wrote in her journal that Ayeshah's husband had joined her in a devotion and a time of praying together every night.

By August, Ayeshah wanted to be baptized, but she also wanted to wait a month because she believed her husband would want to be baptized by then.

The more Ayeshah and Susan studied together, the more excited about sharing her faith Ayeshah became. She asked Susan for booklets and she read the Scriptures daily.

September 30—less than a year after Ayeshah and Susan started studying together—was baptism day!

Susan wrote in her journal: "Lord, I pray that You would be glorified and honored throughout today. I pray for each one being baptized—that they would know Your presence in a special way throughout this day. I pray that Satan 'prowling around like a lion, seeking whom he may devour' would go away empty!"

Ayeshah and her husband were both baptized that glorious day. Susan wrote: "My heart overflows with thanksgiving! . . . You are Almighty God! Master! Tender Shepherd! Oh, Lord, bless Ayeshah and her husband with continued outpouring of Your spirit to encourage their hearts and bind them together as one in You!"

Susan expressed her concern for Ayeshah because of her eagerness to share and because of her great beauty, which puts her in the public eye. Susan wrote: "I pray for her protection. . . . Lord, hide her in the cleft of the rock. Set her on higher ground where they can only see Your glory. Protect her so she can continue being Your witness."

And Ayeshah does continue to share the Lord by her words and actions. She told Susan that a fellow employee saw her when she was wearing a *dupatta*, the long scarf that hangs down the back. For some time Ayeshah had been wearing a cross necklace. The co-worker said, "Oh, I see you took off your cross!"

Ayeshah answered, "Oh, no, I always wear it!"

He replied that he was encouraged by that because he was a Christian, too!

Ayeshah is being used of the Lord in unbelievable ways. Her vibrant and positive stand amazes all who know her. Yet she gives all she does to the Father.

"My faith is a growing process," says Ayeshah. "Through the years, tears, experiences, and joys, it means more and more to me. I clearly remember when Todd baptized me, I couldn't believe how loved I felt. But I was also aware that there was much work that the Lord was going to be doing in me! As Susan quoted to me, 'He who began a good work in you will carry it on to completion' (Phil. 1:6). I am so grateful for that promise because there are so many times when I have fallen back. . . . It is amazing that He still loves me! He does chastise me, but I know even at my worst, He whispers words of comfort to me, and brings me back to Him. I would be *lost* without Him, and so I know that without Him I am nothing."

In God's hands, beautiful and brilliant Ayeshah is a living testimony to the Lord in a land of people who are dying without knowing Jesus Christ as Savior. Her accomplishments are dazzling and truly beyond belief.

Ayeshah is excited that her story is being told. She says, "Share whatever you like. . . . I just don't know what I could say that would be interesting to anyone else." Then she laughs and chides me for being computer illiterate!

It's true, computers baffle me, but I do know God's choice women. And Ayeshah is one of His brightest stars. Even though I can only give you a veiled glimpse of her, she is beyond belief!

WHO'S THE FAIREST OF THEM ALL IN CHINA?

Martha Franks went as a Southern Baptist missionary to China in 1925. For 41 years she served in China and Taiwan.

God used Martha powerfully during those decades. Stories about her have become legends. One of my favorite stories about Martha occurred during the early days of the Japanese occupation and is told in

Martha Franks: One Link in God's Chain by J. Donald McManus.

Martha, who always prayed for me when I wrote, would laugh at her place in this book. She did not consider herself a great beauty. She dearly loved beautiful things, including beautiful clothes. But she did not see the beauty we saw. She glowed. Her love for the Lord and her love for other people was enthralling. Her sense of humor and her quick wit made her eyes dance. She was beautiful inside and out!

But back to the story of "fair Martha." Martha had been asked to join the faculty of the North China Baptist Seminary in Hwanghsien. Only a few years would pass before the invasion of the Japanese, and later, the Communist takeover of all of China.

Hwanghsien fell to the Japanese army without a shot being fired. The invaders drew closer to the seminary. The missionaries decided that women with children, elderly missionaries, ones with furloughs coming soon, and any others who wished to go should leave for America.

Martha had heard horrible tales of barbarous acts of Japanese soldiers. But she prayed, and God told her to stay.

Only six remained: Dr. and Mrs. W. B. Glass, Dr. N. A. Bryan, Dr. Charlie Culpepper, Florence Lide, and Martha.

Life continued much as it had before the coming of the Japanese. The seminary continued to operate.

The missionaries had one advantage over the soldiers. Martha had managed to bring in a portable short-wave radio. Every day at noon there was an English-language broadcast. Martha always listened and passed the news on to the other five. On Monday noon, December 7, Martha heard: "Japan has attacked Pearl Harbor!" The United States had declared war!

Martha rushed to let the others know of the news. Then they waited.

Three days later a large contingent of Japanese soldiers surrounded the seminary. They dropped to the ground with bayonets fixed, and crawled to the buildings. Had Martha not been frightened to death, she would have laughed at all those armed soldiers coming to take just a handful of missionaries who had not even a pocketknife in their possession!

The six missionaries were led to the Culpeppers' house. The soldiers took the first floor and relegated the missionaries to the second floor.

In Charlie Culpepper's room there was a small metal grate in the floor, about one foot square, that was directly over the large stove in the dining room. The captives took turns lying on the floor to watch the soldiers below.

The soldiers talked and laughed. They spoke loudly in Japanese. Then one of the soldiers came to the foot of the stairs and called in Chinese, "Send the young woman down!"

Martha, without a doubt, was the only young woman! What should they do? What could they do?

As the other missionaries prayed, Martha started down the stairs. God walked with her. Hadn't He promised to be with His own, every step of the way?

Martha knew that someone must be in charge. She prayed, "Lord, someone has to be in charge; let it be me. Show me what I should do."

With a deep breath, she opened the door to a dining room filled with Japanese soldiers. She smiled and bowed. The she saw the piano. She walked over, sat down, and began to play.

She played every march, chorus, and tune she had ever played during her kindergarten-teaching days. When she finished those, she played "Silent Night."

As that loveliest of all Christmas carols filled the room—beyond belief—some of the soldiers began humming the tune!

When Martha finished playing "Silent Night," she got up from the piano, and bowed very low to the soldiers. All of them stood and bowed to her!

Without a word, Martha turned and walked back up the stairs. The other missionaries surrounded her, praising God for His love and mercy.

God had opened the eyes of those ferocious soldiers. They had witnessed the beauty—inside and out—of one of God's fairest of them all: Martha Franks.

WHO'S THE FAIREST OF THEM ALL IN ALABAMA?

Julie Smith was chosen to be Miss Alabama in 1999. In the Miss America pageant in September 1999, she was one of the ten semifinalists. But Julie is an unusual young woman. She is the fairest of them all and her heart beats missions!

It all started in a Christian home. Julie declares she started going to church nine months before she was born. Her parents were very involved in church and made sure their children were involved in church. Huffman Baptist Church in Birmingham, Alabama, was second home to the Smiths.

Unfortunately, even Christian families are not immune to problems. Julie's parents divorced when she was six. Her mom, Sharon, raised Julie and her younger twin sisters, Jill and Jennifer.

"Struggles make us stronger," says Julie. "The Book of James talks about finding joy in trials, and that trials help us develop perseverance."

A friend of Julie's was going through the same experience, and Julie was able to encourage that friend. In fact, Julie has the gift of exhortation. She used that gift later, as well, as she served as a counselor at GA® and Acteens® camps in Alabama. Julie encourages teenaged girls to find accountability partners so they can give support to each other. Julie had such a partner. They sent encouraging notes to each other and did Bible studies together.

An extra blessing Julie enjoyed as a teenager was having her mother as her Acteens advisor. Other Acteens leaders, such as the WMU® youth consultant for her state, Sharon Thompson, challenged Julie to be all she could be.

"[They] helped me find joy in following God's will," says Julie. "Acteens instilled in me the importance of studying God's Word and learning how to follow God in little and big things."

Julie did continue to follow the Lord by serving on the Alabama Acteens Panel and as a national (Acteens) Top Teen. During the 1994 National Acteens Convention, she was the star performer in the theme interpretation at each session of the convention. She was fabulous!

All this time, Julie was developing leadership skills and becoming proficient in public speaking. She was gaining poise and grace in any situation. Pretty good training for Miss Alabama. Pretty good training for life!

After becoming Miss Alabama, Julie continued to share her faith in the Lord, and she continued to tell how missions had shaped her life. Some cautioned her strong stand, but Julie never wavered. Being chosen as a semifinalist in the national competition validated her staunch beliefs.

"I learned at a young age," says Julie, "that the only thing that matters in life is that you do your very best and that you honor God in all that you do."

And Julie has strived to do her best. She graduated cum laude from Samford University in Birmingham,

Alabama. In addition, she was an award-winning student journalist at Samford where she won Alabama Associated Press awards as Best Student TV News Reporter and Best Student TV News Anchor. Julie had planned to report after graduation to a major Birmingham television station as a newsroom intern and reporter. She did report to the station. But it was to be interviewed, because she had been crowned Miss Alabama the night before! Put a hold on the TV dream for a while!

The Smith girls made history in the 1999 pageant. It was the first time three sisters—Julie, Jill, and Jennifer—had ever competed together on the state level. The year before, Jill and Jennifer had become the first set of twins to ever compete together in any Miss America preliminary. Imagine, three of the fairest—no, four counting their beautiful mom—in one family!

Julie spoke at the 2000 WMU Annual Meeting in Orlando, Florida. She referred to her years in Mission Friends®, GA, and Acteens. She declared, "WMU is one of the most important parts of my testimony. I don't have the kind of testimony that says, 'Look what God *took* me out of.' I can say, 'Look what God *kept* me out of.' Because of what I learned through WMU, I've felt empowered to do God's work."

Who's the fairest of them all? God's woman—a woman like Julie Smith. There she is: beautiful of face and form, with a heart after God's own choosing!

[1] Michael Avi-Yonah, *Our Living Bible* (New York: McGraw-Hill, 1962), 168.
[2] Ibid.

6

Tipping the Water Jars of Heaven

$\mathcal{G}$od spoke to Job:
"Can you lift up your voice to the clouds,
So that an abundance of water may cover you?
Can you send forth lightnings that they may go
And say to you, 'Here we are'? . . .
Who can count the clouds by wisdom,
Or tip the water jars of the heavens?"
                                    —Job 38:34–35,37 (NASB)

God asked Job lots of questions. Job had none of the answers. All he could say was that God alone did it all and continues to do it all. He is the powerful God Who is beyond belief.

We have learned, however, that when His children call out in anguish, God can tip the water jars of heaven!

TIPPING THE WATER JARS OF HEAVEN AT EKU

Don and Gwen Reece went to Nigeria at the time God (and Nigeria) needed them most. They arrived in the country in 1959 with their two little boys, Kevin and Bryan. Daughter Paige joined the family in 1961. Don tells this story of God's power and protection, even in a difficult time.

Nigeria was granted its independence from Great Britain in 1960. The world looked at the massive nation with its many different tribal groups and numerous languages. It included traditional African religions, as well as Islam and Christianity. English was the national language but it was certainly not enough to unify a country so diverse. Besides all those factors, many felt that Nigerians were inadequately prepared for governing themselves.

Three major tribes exerted the most influence: Yoruba in the Southwest, Igbo [EE-bo] in the Southeast, and Hausa in the North. Many of the Hausas were Muslim.

Igboland was a relatively small territory. The Igbos outgrew their space and began moving into other parts of Nigeria, especially the North, to live and work. Igbos are very industrious and intelligent. They are among the best craftsmen and artisans of the land. Several Igbos rose to top positions in the Nigerian army.

In the 1966 coup, Igbo officers set about "cleansing" the country of leaders they felt were unsuitable. They eliminated a significant number who were not Igbos. This led to retaliation by the Hausas.

This retaliation was devastating to the Igbos, particularly to those in the North. On a Sunday, the Hausas struck in their homes, their churches, and their places of business. Thousands of Igbos were massacred. Leaving everything behind, many others fled to Igboland.

Don Reece remembers a train that arrived in their area from the North. It had been ambushed. Most of the adults on the train had been killed, others were mortally wounded. Many children on the train were petrified with fear, their parents dead, their own safety in jeopardy.

The Hausas often dismiss life's disasters with "It's nothing!" However, Igbos are not so submissive, and the merciless massacres moved the Igbos to secession. A new nation was born: Biafra.

Hopes were high in Biafra. Dr. Chimalum Nwankwo, now an outstanding poet and professor, says that most people of that time "knew that the Igbo people had the potential—the capability—to become a great nation." They were ready to fight for that opportunity.

Most people believed the war would be over in three days. It lasted three years. Newspaper headlines described the "Bloody War." And it was.

For a brief time Igbo soldiers advanced. They came across their border, took the Midwest, and advanced westward. Then hordes of the federal troops started pushing them back into their own territory. In some places, every Igbo was executed.

The Reeces and several other Southern Baptist missionary families lived in the town of Eku, in the Midwest. A Baptist hospital was in Eku, as was a nursing school. Don served as principal of the pastor's training school there. Gwen and the children, along with other missionary mothers and children, were taken to a safer place in the West. Eight missionaries stayed at Eku, including Don.

Many Igbo-speaking people worked at the hospital and were students in the nursing school. They were in danger, as federal troops advanced into the Midwest. A plan was devised in which Don and Harlan Struble, a missionary journeyman, would attempt to drive them to safety, closer to their homeland, in two large vans.

Dr. Martha Hagood, a diminutive Southern Baptist missionary doctor at the hospital, came to Don. "Let me drive the van," she pleaded. "I don't have a wife and three children." Another doctor, Bob Amis, warned them that if they were caught, they would all be killed.

Don confesses that he felt fear for a moment. Then peace flooded over him. Secure, warm, comforting peace led him to say, "If I come back, it's OK; if I don't, it's OK."

The drive to safety began. Thankfully, the nearly impassable roads were dry. The potholes in the roads could swallow a car and wreck a van. Of course, the dry roads would also make it easier for the federal army to follow and overtake the van.

The Christians back in Eku were praying for dry roads so that Don and Harlan could get back safely. Then they asked the Lord for rain so that troop movements would be impossible.

And God tipped the water jars of heaven!

Beyond belief!

It didn't sprinkle. There was no small shower. It poured for 11 days! Everybody in Eku was wading water for days and days.

For a few: safety. But many others filled the roads, walking to get home, trying to find a place of safety.

During this conflict, the American Embassy offered three times to help the missionaries in Eku leave. Each time they answered, "We choose not to go." Don says that God's strength enabled them to do far greater things than they could do in their own strength. His ministry became primarily one of relief work among the Igbo people.

Starvation stopped the war. Inside Biafra and just over the border, *kwashiakor* haunted the villages and roadways, as evidenced by children with sunken eyes and cheeks, spindly legs, every rib showing above swollen bellies. Too many people died.

The people of Eku and those who suffered nearby will never forget those missionaries who stayed with them and were willing to suffer alongside them. Some had bonded forever.

Someone in the US once asked Gwen Reece, "Do you ever forget that those people are black?"

"No," Gwen answered, "I forget I am white."

To some that is beyond belief, but not to a retired missionary couple living in Alabama, whose hearts are still in Igboland.

TIPPING THE WATER JARS OF HEAVEN IN BURKINA FASO

The Dagaari people live in Ghana, Burkina Faso, and Côte d'Ivoire in western Africa. They are some of the poorest people in the world.

Very few of the Dagaari have ever heard of God's love. Not even Scripture portions exist in their language. They are bound by superstition and traditional African religions. How can they be reached? How can they hear and understand that God loves them?

An unusual person is needed to reach the Dagaari, and some miraculous happenings are needed for a spiritual breakthrough.

Enter the person: Lynn Kennedy, who serves as the International Mission Board's strategy coordinator for evangelizing the Dagaari.

Lynn's first breakthrough came when she was introduced to an important chief, Some Emmanuel. He is the regional chief of the Bapla region. He is responsible for offering sacrifices to gain the approval of the Dagaari gods that are believed to oversee planting, cultivating, rainfall, and other weather changes. Some Emmanuel has great influence. At least 20 villages are in his domain, each with 20 to 200 people.

Lynn met Some Emmanuel through his niece, Louis. He accepted Lynn as a member of his family. He says, "Lynn is like my daughter. Pray God will keep her here a long time—and me, too!"[1]

Lynn very wisely asked Some Emmanuel's permission to share the truth about God with the Dagaari; he agreed. Not only that, he gathers his people and tells them to listen to the white woman who "speaks the truth."

Some Emmanuel has not accepted the Lord as his personal Savior—yet. But already he is opening doors in his region, and Lynn expects him to open doors to the nearly quarter-million other Dagaaris. Some Emmanuel unlocks the doors, and Lynn goes in with the powerful truth of the gospel. During the very first evangelistic meeting in 1999, 25 people accepted Christ. The breakthroughs have come because of Lynn's patient, hard work—and God's mighty power.

The Dagaaris are a superstitious and private people. They do not readily accept strangers. They consider themselves to be *vitalistes,* which means they claim transcendental synthesis between experience, intuition, mystical conscience, and the occult.[2]

How in the world is Lynn accepted by these people? As Emmanuel's "adopted" daughter, the people listen to her. And with Louis translating for her, the people can understand.

But in one Dagaari village, God intervened by tipping the water jars of heaven. The village chief, listening carefully to Lynn, pointed to the withered fields.

"The crops are dry and my people are hungry," he said. He asked her to pray for rain. She did. Three hours later the sky opened and rain poured on that arid land all night long! Beyond belief!

Lynn keeps on praying and working. She prays that the Holy Spirit will pour down on the dry hearts of the Dagaaris and they will come to know the Lord.

TIPPING THE WATER JARS OF HEAVEN IN CAMBODIA

In July 1997 a violent coup ousted the democratically

elected first prime minister in Cambodia. Several hundred people died during heavy shelling in the capital city of Phnom Penh. But during those perilous days, God miraculously protected the lives of many Christian believers.

The second day of fighting was a Sunday. The intensity of the conflict prevented families from attending worship services. Instead they had their own private services in their homes.

One family was singing hymns during the bombardment when someone rushed in to say that a shell had landed nearby. Fires were burning in the surrounding areas. In fact, their own house was beginning to burn!

They cried out to the Father for His divine intervention. As soon as they began to pray, God tipped the water jars of heaven! A heavy rain descended and drenched the fires. They were protected from tragic loss. Beyond belief!

Elsewhere in the city, two separate families from two different churches experienced a similar miracle. The families lived on opposite sides of the street. Shelling ignited fierce fires in the wooden shanties and storefront homes along their road. As the fire advanced, burning everything in its path, the two families began to pray.

God again tipped his water jars and quenched the flames on both sides of the street. God had a city map of Phnom Penh, and He knew exactly where the rain was needed to stop the fires!

TIPPING THE WATER JARS OF HEAVEN IN LONDON
Helen Jean Parks tells the story of Larry in her book, *Holding the Ropes*.

Larry, a missionary journeyman in Malawi, had been seriously injured on an outing with young people. He had dived from an eight-foot rock into water only two feet deep.

Larry suffered from fractured and dislocated vertebrae, skull lacerations, and great respiratory distress because of the swelling. His spinal column was not severed, thank the Lord, but he was running a high fever. The decision was made to transfer Larry to an American hospital that was better equipped to handle his injuries. Larry began a miraculous 38-hour flight to Dallas's Baylor hospital. Malawi's president gave special permission for 2 of the country's 20 doctors to accompany the young paralyzed man who was fighting for his life.

The British Overseas Airways plane reached London. The tower warned that heavy fog cloaked the airport and the ceiling was below minimum. The control tower advised the pilot to fly to Scotland.

That would have meant a long overland trip back to London, then a search for another flight to the United States. Could Larry survive that?

The captain of the airplane announced, "I'll give it five more minutes." But there was no chance the fog would lift. It was dropping, not lifting.

People in many parts of the world were praying for Larry. Southern Baptist missionary Roy G. Davidson Jr., who was traveling with the injured journeyman, tells what happened next: "As we were on the final approach, the fog rose to the minimum 900 meters with 200 meters of visibility. No one in the plane or the tower could believe it. The minute we touched down, it dropped again and no more planes could land."[3]

God had turned those water jars right side up and had brought a few meters of fog right up with them!

Larry made it, and God made it happen. It was beyond belief!

82

TIPPING THE WATER JARS OF HEAVEN IN INDONESIA

Bill O'Brien is retired director of Beeson School of Divinity's Global Center. His wife, Dellanna, author of *Beyond Belief!*, vol. 1 was executive director/treasurer of Woman's Missionary Union® from 1989 to 1999. Bill shares this wonderful story about a special miracle that happened many years ago when he, Dellanna, and their three children—Denise, Erin, and Ross—were Southern Baptist missionaries in Indonesia.

Twenty-six missionaries who lived in central Java had attended their annual prayer retreat in the beautiful mountains outside of Yogyakarta. The retreat had been a time of spiritual renewal that was beyond their greatest expectations.

A few weeks passed and missionaries Von and Marge Worton invited the O'Brien family to their home in Poerwokerto to spend Easter with them. The Wortons were the only missionaries living in that area of central Java at that time.

Marge's mother, Norma Jones, had come to visit the Wortons from Phoenix, Arizona, for a few months. The families talked endlessly about the retreat and the blessing it had been. The afterglow was still lingering in their hearts and minds.

On the Friday before Easter, Norma, Marge, Von, and their four-year-old Vance, along with Bill, Dellanna, Denise, Erin, and Ross, went on an outing to Ketenggar Falls, near Poerwokerto.

The falls were at the end of a boxed canyon. In order to see the falls, they waded into the river, which was not even to their knees.

They left their outer garments on a huge boulder in the middle of the river. Then they waded down the river a good distance to a large pool. The pool was at the bottom of the cascading water that was falling from the high mountain above.

The two young boys, Ross O'Brien and Vance Worton, were dragging behind everyone else, playing as they came. The rest of the group reached the pool and were enjoying themselves in the clear waters.

Then Von looked up and commented about the heavy rain clouds over the mountain. It wasn't long until the lovely pristine falls turned to an ugly brown and were suddenly flooding over the sides of the mountain. The two families knew what that meant: Get back to the entry point as fast as you can!

The group had not waded far when the water became deeper. The river, instead of being calm, was churning at a furious pace.

Vance and Ross were now leading the pack, which probably was the key to their survival. When they finally reached the boulder where they had left their clothes, the huge rock was covered with muddy water. At this point it was much harder for the group to keep their footing in the fierce rush.

But, praise the Lord, the little flock included Von Worton, former football player, a big man of great strength. Von first helped Dellanna and Denise to the bank and they received the two little boys and Erin as Von fished them out.

Norma, Marge's mother, was holding onto a big rock that was partly above the water. Marge and Bill were grasping the underside of another rock to keep from being swept away.

Von came back into the torrent after delivering the children. He positioned himself against a boulder and yelled to Norma, "Let go!"

Norma was hurtled along by the raging tide. Von reached out and grabbed her and by sheer brute force got her to land.

Bill had noticed as they went to the falls that this seemed to be the only place on the crowded island of

Java where there were no people. It was absolutely desolate. But now they suddenly noticed a Javanese man on a swinging footbridge over the river, watching the drama taking place below. As Von went back into the river once again, the Javanese man came down and joined him.

Von shouted to Bill, "Let go! I'll try to catch you when you come downstream!"

Bill confesses, "I am not a good swimmer, and I was mortified to let go!"

By this time both Bill and Marge were certain that not everyone would make it. They thought they remembered another waterfall downstream and were fearful that they would be washed over it. The water kept rising and the current grew swifter.

Finally, Bill let go. Von shouted, "Keep your head up!" He was afraid Bill would hit his head on one of the big rocks.

Von caught Bill and was immediately aided by the Javanese man. No sooner had Bill been caught than Marge was swept from the rock. Von turned and was able to swoop her up as she came by.

Bill linked arms with the Javanese man, Von, and Marge, and they made their way to safety! They gratefully thanked the man for his help, then their families tearfully and joyfully surrounded them.

Bill remembers, "We stood together in one glob of hugs, crying and praising the Lord. Almost spontaneously, we broke into song, 'God is so good . . .'"

They made their way onto the suspension bridge. They looked back toward the waterfall, which no longer was a pristine cascade, but had become a deadly flood leaping down the sides of the mountain. Most of the gigantic boulders were now completely under the water.

Bill took pictures to mark the day. However, he says, "No picture is necessary to remind us of the scene itself, of the strength granted to Von in a moment of crisis, nor of the appearance of the hand of the Lord in the form of a Javanese peasant farmer."

The morning after the miraculous delivery, Bill was led to Psalm 116: "I love the Lord, for he heard my voice; he heard my cry for mercy. Because he turned his ear to me, I will call on him as long as I live. The cords of death entangled me, the anguish of the grave came upon me; I was overcome by trouble and sorrow. Then I called on the name of the Lord: 'O Lord, save me!'" (Psalm 116:1–4 NIV).

And God did save them all. As the psalmist said, "He delivered them from death, their eyes from tears, their feet from stumbling, that they might walk before the Lord in the land of the living" (Psalm116:8–9).

Bill adds, "And a dear lesson in it all was that our security is not so much in holding on as it is in letting go."

Beyond belief—they let go, and God lifted them out of the floods of His water jars!

TIPPING THE WATER JARS OF HEAVEN ONTO THE WHOLE EARTH

In Genesis 6 the heart of man is exposed: "The Lord saw how great man's wickedness on the earth had become, and that every inclination of the thoughts of his heart was only evil all the time. The Lord was grieved that He had made man on the earth, and His heart was filled with pain. So the Lord said, 'I will wipe mankind, whom I have created, from the face of the earth—men and animals, and creatures that move along the ground, and birds of the air—for I am grieved that I have made them.' But Noah found favor in the eyes of the Lord" (Gen. 6:5–8 NIV).

Kenneth A. Matthews in his commentary notes that society at the time of Noah had decayed beyond recovery.[4] God saw it and was grieved over what had become of His divine creation. He had breathed His own breath into man.

Genesis 6:5 sadly declares that every inclination of the thoughts of man's heart was only evil all the time. The whole world was polluted with sin.

God knew His making of man was no error. The problem was what man had made of himself. In order to salvage humanity, God had to cleanse the earth.

So God said, "I will wipe out mankind. . . and animals, and creatures that move along the ground, and birds of the air" (Gen. 6:7).

Everything was to be obliterated. The end. But God saw Noah. Praise God, he saw Noah, and Noah found favor in God's eyes.

Now why did Noah receive God's gracious favor? Matthews believes it had to do with Noah's righteous conduct. Ezekiel also commented on Noah's righteous behavior much later (Ezek. 14:14,20).[5]

Genesis 6:9 claims that Noah was "blameless" and "walked with God." The writer of Hebrews mentions Noah's obedient "fear" as faith that resulted in a saving righteousness (Heb. 11:7). God told Noah about His decision (Gen. 6:13) and immediately told him to build an ark (Gen. 6:14).

So Noah was forewarned. No doubt he warned others, and they would have nothing to do with it! Even so, Noah persisted. He listened to God's instructions, which were carefully spelled out (Gen. 6:14–16). We have no record of his saying to Mrs. Noah, "This is no canoe, it's a whopper!" but perhaps he did.

I would love to know how he rounded up all the animals, especially the crawling creatures and the birds! We do know that God helped him. Some must have scurried on at the last minute!

And how in the world did Noah ever gather up enough food to keep everybody and everything fed for so long? All we know is that Noah did everything just as God commanded him (Gen. 6:22).

When God told Noah to get into the ark, Noah did it (Gen. 7: 5). And the flood began. "The springs of the great deep burst forth, and the floodgates of the heavens were opened. And rain fell on the earth forty days and forty nights" (Gen. 7: 11–12).

The Lord shut the door to the ark. Genesis 7:16 says so. All outside the ark went to a watery grave. For 40 days it rained, and the earth was inundated. Even the highest mountains were below the waters (Gen. 7:19).

Finally the waters calmed and began to recede. The ark grounded on the mountains of Ararat (Gen. 8:4). It may have grounded at 17,000 feet! The important thing is, it grounded, and all aboard were saved.

God has kept the promise He made to Noah and all mankind. There has never been another flood to wipe out mankind. God sent His rainbow as a seal. Each time a Christian believer spots the rainbow after the rain, he or she should thank God for bringing us through the waters—waters truly beyond belief!

[1] Heidi Soderstrom, "When the Chief Speaks, the People Listen," *the Commission*, April 2000, 34.
[2] Ibid.
[3] Helen Jean Parks, *Holding the Ropes* (Nashville: Broadman & Holman Publishers, 1983), 12.
[5] Kenneth A. Matthews, *New American Commentary*, vol. 1A, *Genesis* (Nashville: Broadman & Holman Publishers, 1995), 339.
[6] Ibid., 346.

7

Thy Word Have I Hid in My Heart and Various Other Places

THY WORD HAVE I HID IN MY PILLOW

Violet Wood, in her gripping volume called *Great Is the Company*, tells this incredible story of Adoniram Judson from the pages of missions history.

Adoniram wrote in his journal: "November 1, 1819 . . . [I am] beginning to query whether it is prudent to go boldly on."

Adoniram bowed his head as he thought of his six years in Burma. It had cost him dearly—the loss of his first child, the declining health of his wife, Ann.

And what had he accomplished? Three Burmese converts who were so afraid of the emperor's anger that they asked for secret baptism by night.

He had learned to read, write, and speak Burmese, though he felt he had only scratched the surface of knowing the language. And he was progressing on the translation of the New Testament into Burmese.

A new assistant, James Coleman, had come to Burma 6 months earlier. He was chafing under all the restrictions they were facing. He urged Adoniram to go to see King Bagyidaw and ask for tolerance. If the king refused, James felt they should leave Burma.

Adoniram agreed and the two men set off to Ava where the king's palace was located. The 350-mile journey took them 35 days by inland river waters.

Adoniram and James reached the splendid palace with its flawless white marble and jewel-studded doors. They brought a petition asking for favor from the king and permission to preach their religion, exempt of molestation by the government. They also brought tracts and a beautiful six-volume Bible in English as a gift to the king.

When they were received by the king, he took the tract and read it: "There is one eternal God, beside him there is no God."

It infuriated the king, and Adoniram and James were abruptly dismissed.

When they returned to Rangoon, Adoniram was ready to quit, but the three converts would not hear of it. Moreover, the little church began to grow. Adoniram worked even harder on the translation and finished the New Testament.

Later the Judsons moved to Ava to begin a new work. Without much warning, war broke out between Great Britain and Burma.

All white males were arrested and thrown into the death prison at Ava. Adoniram stayed 11 months in the windowless cellar, which was always 100°F. Irons on the ankles and fetters on the wrists allowed the swarms of mosquitoes to feast on the prisoners. Adoniram would have died there if Ann had not come daily with food and water.

Violet Wood says, "No greater insight into the motivation of this man's life, his will to endure and serve, can be given than the fact that his concern for his wife, his newborn baby, and the manuscript translation of the New Testament was greater than his concern for himself."[1]

Adoniram's concern for the manuscript surfaced as soon as Ann came to the prison.

"Where is the New Testament manuscript?" he asked, worriedly.

Ann confided that she had wrapped it in a cloth and buried it under the house. Adoniram warned that it was the rainy season, fearing that the manuscript would mold and rot.

They thought of another plan. "I will make it into a pillow for you!" said Ann. So she took the manuscript and sewed it up into a pillow so hard and uncomfortable that even the jailers didn't want it. Adoniram put it under his head every night.[2]

When the prisoners were moved into an inner prison, Adoniram's pillow was given to one of the jailers and Adoniram received a better one. As soon as he could, Adoniram offered to trade his "good" pillow for the "hard" pillow. The jailer jumped at the trade, probably thinking, "What fools these white men are!"[3]

When the prisoners were driven on a death march to another place, one of the guards grabbed the pillow and tore into it. But Ann had done a good job and the jailer thought it was but rags. He threw it onto the trash heap.

Adoniram wept so wildly for his dirty pillow that the prisoners in front and in back of him decided that he had lost his mind. But the jailers ignored Adoniram and forced their chained gang to begin their 10-mile death march.

The march was beyond belief. Begging for water, under the scorching tropical sun, on bleeding feet, some finally reached the prison at Oung-pen-lah. Adoniram, half-dead (many had died on the march) remained in the prison for 7 months, waiting for his execution.

But God had other plans.

A royal order came through. Adoniram was loosed from his chains and sent with guards to the Burmese camp to translate and interpret. They informed him that his wife and baby were safe. When he asked about his pillow, they scoffed and couldn't have cared less.

Adoniram served in the Burmese camp until the war ended. Then the general of the British army had Adoniram sent to him because of his skills in the language.

The peace treaty was signed and Adoniram returned to Rangoon on March 21, 1826. The faithful Burmese Christians were waiting to greet their teacher. He was gaunt and limped painfully. His 21 months of misery had left scars that he would carry to his grave.

One of the greeters in Rangoon was Moung Ing, who had been one of the first three converts. He cried, "Twice the almond tree has borne its fruit and still my heart had mourned for you. All I had was the words of your heart to comfort me. No garment of yours to touch, no grave to bless with my tears. Even yet I have the foul pillow on which your blessed head lay."

"What pillow?" asked Adoniram, barely able to whisper.

"The torn pillow. From the prison yard. I picked it up and held it to my heart the day I reached Ava to visit you. The dreadful day I found they had all gone and you with them, to the place of death."[4]

The faithful Moung Ing took Adoniram to the place where the pillow was. Adoniram went to his knees as he tore away the hard cotton and dried palm leaves. And there in his trembling hands was the dear manuscript!

At last Adoniram had what he loved most: his wife, his baby, and the translation of the New Testament!

More tragedy was ahead, however. When Adoniram went to Ava on mission business, Ann was struck with Indian fever. Sadly, she died and was buried two weeks before the news even reached her husband. The baby, Maria, succumbed as well.

Left with only his manuscript, Adoniram poured himself into translating the Old Testament. By December 29, 1835, he had finished the last page and the complete Burmese Bible went to press. His monumental accomplishment began to open the doors of Buddha's stronghold.

God's Word survived odds beyond belief!

THY WORD HAVE I FOUND AS MY BREAD WRAPPER

God has promised that His Word will not return to Him without results. But how does a missionary get the Scriptures to an unreached people group? Phillip and Karen Brown are missionaries to the Sereer people in Senegal, in western Africa. They found a way.

As the Browns observed the daily life and routine of the Sereer, they discovered that most of them go to the weekly markets near their villages. It is a social gathering as well as a time for buying. They meet their friends, their relatives, and the village leaders. They exchange news and information. They see everybody because almost every Sereer person goes to the market within walking distance of his or her home at least once a month.

The Browns decided on an innovative strategy. As they put it, God's strategy is to "send the gospel to the people where they are." The Browns' call is to take the gospel to the Sereers where they are—in this case, at the market. So it makes sense to take the

Scriptures to the market—to saturate the market with God's Word.

How? Every market sells bread. How about combining the bread in the market with the Bread of life—the Scriptures? So the Bread of Life Ministry was born.

Every local bread vendor going to the weekly market is supplied with free bread wrappers, which they are pleased to receive. Every bread wrapper has on it the Bread of Life logo. It also includes the location of a Bread of Life distributor within the market. This distributor has a booth, and the booth is marked with the Bread of Life logo. People who are interested can find the booth easily.

Each Bread of Life distributor is a believer—an evangelist/church planter. In other words, he will be able to answer any questions and explain any materials, and he knows how to share the gospel. He will be familiar with the materials at the booth.

What are the materials?

1. *Storylines.* These are sheets containing colorfully illustrated Old Testament stories. There are 14 Storylines available in printed form and on cassette. The Storylines tell the Old Testament stories chronologically to build a person's understanding of Who God is. Then when the person is presented with the gospel of Christ, the Holy Spirit can move.

2. *Daily Bread Scripture Cards.* A card is awarded to a person or group of people who collect a complete set of sheets from a Storyline. Also, each time anyone learns and recites the story to a distributor, that person is given a Daily Bread Scripture Card.

   In addition, each time anyone teaches the s t o r y to others in a village and those who are taught the story can recite it to the distributor, the teacher and the learner are both awarded a Daily Bread Scripture Card.

The Scripture cards are valuable possessions and are used as daily devotional cards. As a person collects each series of Daily Bread Scripture Cards, he or she can begin another Storyline or choose a Scripture cassette or a personal copy of the New Testament.

3. *The Jesus Film.* When the majority of people in a compound or house, including the leadership, completes the Storylines and agrees to view the *Jesus* film, they can receive a radio cassette player at the first viewing of the film. Out of the viewing, it is hoped that many will believe and that the believers will begin to meet together, resulting in a church.

Members of a nearby house church can go to the viewing of the *Jesus* film, also. If there are believers or seekers that want to continue to study, laymen from the existing church can begin planting a new church there.

4. *Praise Songs, Testimonies, Broadcasts.* The radio cassette players can be used to begin a discipleship study. Using the players, Sereers can listen to and learn praise songs written and performed by Sereers in other churches. They can play testimonies from Sereer believers. They can listen to the Bread of Life Ministry broadcast. The Browns have kept in mind that most Sereers are oral learners.

Considering the number of markets and people needed to work the booths, the Bread of Life Ministry is a giant imaginative vision that can have a great impact on the Sereer people. It can be used as a model for other unreached people groups. It is beyond belief that a bread wrapper can be the beginning of such a ministry that shares God's Word!

The Browns' goal is to have 200 market ministries set up this year. May it be so!

THY WORD HAVE I HID BENEATH MY CLOTHES

Thousands of people all over the world have read Corrie ten Boom's *The Hiding Place*. The book broke the hearts of thousands of readers. It also opened their eyes to the atrocities of the Holocaust and the horrors of the German concentration camps.

The riveting characters of *The Hiding Place* were the two sisters, Corrie and Betsie ten Boom. The crime that sent them to prison, and ultimately a German concentration camp, was hiding Jews in their home in Haarlem, Holland.

Their courage, their tremendous faith in God during the worst of times, and their dependence on the Bible—all are beyond belief. Likewise, the story of the hiding of God's Word is no legend; it is true and it is truly beyond belief. Corrie tells this story in *The Hiding Place*.

After their arrest, Corrie, Betsie, and cattle cars full of women reached their final destination: Ravensbruck, the dreaded, notorious concentration and extermination camp for women, deep inside Germany.

As the sick, starving, exhausted women stumbled toward the camp, Corrie could feel her Bible bumping between her shoulder blades. She had made a cloth bag for it, tied the bag around her neck, and hidden it beneath her clothes. She had managed to hold on to it through the agonizing journey toward Ravensbruck. Through its pages God had spoken to the hearts of so many. How they prayed they could somehow hide it and keep it.

After three days of waiting outdoors at the camp, they were marched to the processing center. When they entered the building, they saw the line of women approaching a desk where each had to surrender her pillowcase, her blanket, and any other possessions she had. The pile was becoming a mountain.

A little further along, each woman had to strip off every scrap of clothing and throw it onto another pile. Then she had to walk naked past a dozen leering SS men into the shower room. After the shower, each woman put on a thin prison dress and a pair of shoes. Nothing more.

Corrie thought, "Betsie needs her sweater. Her cough is worse and she needs the vitamins we have saved." But most of all, they needed the Bible! How could they survive in such a place without the Bible?

But Corrie knew there was no way—no humanly possible way—to get by the guards with any of those things. She began to pray: "Dear God, you have hidden your precious book through checkpoints and inspections. "

She felt Betsie press against her. A guard was passing by and Corrie begged him to let them go to the toilets. He jerked his head in the direction of the shower room.

It was empty, waiting for the next bunch of 50 frightened women to be led in. When Corrie asked the guard at the door about the toilets, he told her to use the drain holes.

When they entered, the guard stayed outside. Corrie spotted a pile of old wooden benches in a far corner. Slimy and mildewed, crawling with cockroaches, those benches seemed to Corrie to be the furniture of heaven! She grabbed Betsie's sweater, untied her Bible bag, and stuffed it all, along with the vitamins, under the benches. Then she and Betsie rejoined their group. A few minutes later, they were herded back into the showers.

They stood beneath the flow of icy water as long as it lasted. Then they huddled around the heap of prison dresses, looking for an approximate fit. Corrie found a long-sleeved dress for Betsie that would cover the blue sweater. She found another for herself then reached behind the benches for the bag. She put the bag beneath the dress, tying the strings around her neck.

You could see the bulge the sweater and Bible made from a mile away. Corrie flattened it as best she could, pushing and tugging, but there was no way to conceal it beneath the thin cotton dress.

An unbelievable feeling came over her: It didn't matter. This was God's business. All she had to do was walk straight ahead.

As they came out of the shower room, the SS men ran their hands over each prisoner, front, back, and sides. The woman ahead of Corrie was searched three times. Behind her, Betsie was searched. But no one touched Corrie.

When the two sisters arrived at Barracks 8, they brought "not only the Bible, but a new knowledge of the power of Him whose story it was!"[5]

Every day grew harder—such misery, such suffering. Corrie declared, "Our Bible was the center of an ever-widening circle of help and hope. Like waifs clustered around a blazing fire, we gathered about it, holding our hearts to its warmth and light. The blacker the night around us grew, the brighter and truer and more beautiful burned the word of God. 'Who will separate us from the love of Christ? Shall tribulation, or distress, or persecution, or famine, or nakedness, or peril, or sword? Nay, in all these things we are more than conquerors through him that loved us.'"[6]

Corrie watched the faces of the women in their barracks as Betsie read. She knew that "more than conquerors" was not just a promise for the future. They were already more than conquerors, experiencing it minute by minute.

Corrie marveled anew at the truths of God's Word. It seemed that it had just been written for her.

When Corrie and Betsie were moved to a different barracks, an added misery awaited them—fleas! But the fleas kept their barracks guards away. Inside Barracks 28, they were free! They were able to have "services" with even more women. They were able to share the riches of God's Holy Word.

God's Word was light in the dark and horrendous heart of hell on earth. Man's depravity was unbelievable, but God Himself was there, loving and comforting His children. What a life-giving blessing, beyond belief.

THY WORD WAS HIDDEN BY THE DARKNESS OF MY MIND

Can you imagine having the Scriptures in your hands but not understanding it? That's a fact of life for many in the world.

One of my favorite Lillian Isaacs stories is about a woman who could not read. As a missionary, Miss Lillian pioneered Christian literacy missions ministries. I "sat at Miss Lillian's feet" as we traveled to district WMU® meetings in Alabama several years ago. I drank in her wonderful stories. Miss Lillian, a master literacy teacher, told of teaching one woman to read. The woman testified, "When I wake up now at night, I just get up and get my Bible and read myself some."

Blessed are those who teach people to read.

My heartfelt appreciation goes out to Bible translators who make the Word plain in the many languages of the world. People understand God's love better when they read it in the languages of their hearts.

Perhaps it all began on a road that goes down from Jerusalem to Gaza. William Barclay, in his commentary on Acts, says this road from Jerusalem went through Bethlehem and Hebron and joined the main road to Egypt just south of Gaza. The traffic of half the world went this route.[7]

Along this road, in his chariot, came the Ethiopian eunuch.

Also, along this very same road, God sent Philip, the evangelist.

During this time, Ethiopia was an object of curiosity to the Greeks and Romans. Ethiopian kings were considered incarnations of the sun god and were ceremonial rulers. The real power—the administration—belonged to the powerful queen mothers, who had the title of "the Candace."[8]

The Ethiopian eunuch today would probably be called the minister of finance. He had been on a pilgrimage to Jerusalem and was perhaps a "God-fearing" Gentile who believed in the God of Israel, but was not a full convert to Judaism.

Many beyond-belief facts are part of this story. For instance, how did the eunuch get the scroll he was reading? Perhaps they could be purchased—for a price. Certainly the eunuch had "the price." And he could read it. He just couldn't understand it.

At the beginning of the scriptural account, we read that "an angel of the Lord said to Philip, 'Go south to the road—the desert road—that goes down from Jerusalem to Gaza'" (Acts 8:26 NIV). And Philip did. The angel's orders were brief and to the point. Philip didn't question, he simply did as he was told. And he saw the Ethiopian eunuch, who was sitting in his chariot and reading from the Book of Isaiah.

A word about the chariot. I have always pictured an outrageously beautiful and spacious buggy drawn by six snow-white horses. In reality, it was probably an ox-drawn covered wagon. Perhaps a retinue of high-ranking official servants followed the wagon on foot. This slow-moving wagon was not difficult to catch on the only road around. (Of course, even if it had been speedy, the Lord could have helped Philip catch it anyway!)

Acts 8:29 spotlights the Holy Spirit: "The Spirit told Philip, 'Go to that chariot and stay near it.'" Again, Philip did as he was directed.

John B. Polhill says that it was not by accident that the eunuch was reading Isaiah. Of all the Old Testament readings, Isaiah gives the greatest hope for one like the Ethiopian eunuch (see Isa. 56:3–8). Isaiah promises a name better than sons and daughters, an "everlasting name that will not be cut off" (Isa. 56:5 NIV).[9] The eunuch never dreamed that he was about to experience that promise!

And Philip didn't have a clue about how God was going to use him. But still he ran up to the chariot— actually, the slow-moving wagon—and began to trot alongside. He heard the eunuch reading aloud from Isaiah 53. It was the natural thing (being led by the Holy Spirit) for Philip to ask the eunuch, "Do you understand what you are reading?" (Acts 8:30).

The eunuch answered, "How can I . . . unless someone explains it to me?" (Acts 8:31).

Philip's heart must have leaped within him! Explaining that the Christ, the Lord Jesus, was the Suffering Servant of Isaiah 53, Who had so recently been led like a sheep to the slaughter at the Cross—this was what Christians had been sharing since the Resurrection!

So Philip climbed up into the wagon and told the Ethiopian "the good news about Jesus" (Acts 8:35).

No doubt, Philip followed his sharing of the gospel (as any good preacher would do) with an invitation to believe in the Lord Jesus Christ.

Can you believe that about that very time they reached a pool of water? The eunuch exclaimed, "Look, here is water. Why shouldn't I be baptized?" (Acts 8:36). Barriers of all kinds fell as Philip baptized the Ethiopian. Then two more beyond belief happenings occurred. First, the Spirit of the Lord took Philip away (Acts 8:39). Some versions say that Philip was "snatched" up by the Spirit. His work was completed with the Ethiopian.

The other happening concerned the eunuch. Later church fathers claim he became a missionary in Ethiopia. Irenaeus in his *Heresies* says he evangelized Arabia and the Red Sea coastal areas as well.[10]

God, using Philip and His Holy Word, made major progress toward fulfilling Christ's commission to take the gospel to the ends of the earth.

That is beyond belief!

[1] Violet Wood, *Great Is the Company* (New York: Friendship Press, 1966), 75.
[2] J. M. Hull, *Judson the Pioneer* (Philadelphia: American Baptist Publication Society, 1913), 158.
[3] Ibid., 159.
[4] Wood, *Great Is the Company*, 77.
[5] Corrie ten Boom, *The Hiding Place* (Boston: G. K. Hall & Co., 1973), 346.
[6] Ibid., 349.
[7] William Barclay, *The Acts of the Apostles* (Philadelphia: Westminster Press, 1976), 68.
[8] John B. Polhill, *The New American Commentary*, vol. 26, *Acts* (Nashville: Broadman & Holman Publishers, 1992), 223.
[9] Ibid., 224.
[10] Ibid., 227.

8

But She Had to Go

*W*e often hear exciting stories of men who are called by God and answer against all odds, against all common sense, in times of great personal danger. But how often do we hear these kinds of stories about women?

Are women called by God? Of course they are.

Do women answer against all odds? Of course they do.

Do women sometimes answer when it is not good sense? Oh, yes.

Do women answer even if it could mean great personal danger? They have and will continue to do so.

If you have a dime, I have a dozen such stories!

ELISABETH ELLIOT IN THE JUNGLES OF ECUADOR

In 1955 five young men dreamed an impossible dream: Nate Saint, Roger Youderian, Ed McCully, Pete Fleming, and Jim Elliot. They had made contact with an isolated tribe—the Aucas—deep in the rain forest of Ecuador. Elisabeth Elliot, wife of Jim Elliot, has written their compelling story in her classic book, *Through Gates of Splendor*.

The first missionary to go into Auca territory in 1667—a Jesuit priest—was speared to death. For the next 200 years nobody bothered the Aucas. Then men searching for rubber came in 1875. For 50 years these men burned Auca homes and raped, tortured, and enslaved the people. No wonder the Aucas hated the white man.

But five white men truly believed that Christian love could conquer that hatred, and they were dedicated to the task. They went to Ecuador, in northwestern South America, with their wives and children.

Nate Saint brought Marj, son Philip, and daughter Kathie; Roger Youderian brought Barbara, son Jerry, and daughter Bethy; Ed McCully brought Marilou and sons Steve and Michael; Pete Fleming brought Olive, his bride; and Jim Elliot brought Betty (Elisabeth) and daughter Valerie.

The team originally consisted of only Pete Fleming and Jim Elliot. But they believed completely that God wanted them to carry the gospel to the Aucas. They watched and waited to find God's plan.

Pete wrote in his journal: "The thought scares me at times, but I am ready. We have believed God for miracles, and this may include the Aucas."[1]

Then Ed McCully went to Ecuador and the team numbered three. Nate Saint, a Missionary Aviation Fellowship pilot, was the fourth to join the Auca team. Wasn't that just like the Lord to give them a pilot! Saint had gone to Ecuador in 1948 and had been flying for the missionaries in Ecuador since then. His wife, Marj, was his right hand, maintaining radio checks with their shortwave radio as he flew the jungles.

Finally, the Auca team was completed with Roger Youderian. He had been in Ecuador since 1945, working with the Jivaro Indians, a group known all over the world for their head-shrinking expertise.

The five men prayed and planned about the best way to reach the Aucas. They gathered every bit of information they could find.

One amazing bit of help came their way. An Auca teenager, Dayuma, had survived a family feud and escaped. She was living with Quichua Indians. Dayuma taught the missionaries the customs of the Aucas and some vocabulary. What a blessing!

She also advised them, "Never, never trust them; they may appear friendly and then they will turn around and kill."[2]

The men set their faces toward these people who were in darkness. For three months they made weekly flights over Auca settlements at a place they called Terminal City. They dropped gifts from a line they suspended from Nate's little yellow airplane. The Aucas sometimes gave gifts in return, such as a feathered headdress, fruit, and the like.

Finally, on January 3, 1956, Ed, Jim, and Roger were flown in by Nate to "Palm Beach" in Auca territory. Pete and Nate joined them later, flying out each evening and returning each morning. And they waited for the Aucas to come.

On Friday, January 6, three Aucas stepped out of the jungle—a man and two women. They stayed for several hours.

The men knew they were where God had led them. They knew the cost could be everything. However, the question of personal safety was wholly and totally irrelevant.

Sunday, January 8: Nate Saint flew into Palm Beach. He called Marj at 12:30 to tell her that from the air he had spotted Aucas on their way to the clearing. He promised to contact her at 4:30 that afternoon.

At 4:30 Marj Saint waited eagerly at the radio.

Silence.

She contacted the other wives—and they waited. Nobody got much sleep that night.

By 7:00 the next morning, Johnny Keenan, a Missionary Aviation Fellowship colleague, was flying to the landing spot. Nate had pointed out the Palm Beach site to him earlier.

Keenan saw the plane—the fabric had been stripped away from the body. He saw no sign of any of the five men.

During the following week fellow missionaries, American and Ecuadorian military personnel, and even other Indians organized search parties. The five were found. It had been a massacre. The missionaries had been speared to death with the hardwood lances of the Aucas.

The tragedy shook the world. Just months after the deaths of the five missionaries, Elisabeth Elliot wrote the martyrs' story in *Through Gates of Splendor*. It has become a classic that has inspired hundreds of thousands of people. From all over the world have come testimonies of lives changed by what happened on Palm Beach.

And what of those five young widows? They turned to God's Word: "All this has come upon us, yet have we not forgotten Thee. . . . Our heart is not turned back, neither have our steps declined from Thy way, though Thou hast sore broken us in the place of dragons, and covered us with the shadow of death" (Ps. 44:17–19 KJV).

Almost immediately, the women declared that the work must continue. And each was ready—no, compelled—to go.

Barbara Youderian returned to the Jivaro Indians with her two young children.

Elisabeth Elliot and her ten-month-old Valerie went to their former Quichua Indian station to continue the work.

Marj Saint began new work in Quito, Ecuador.

Marilou McCully went to the United States for the birth of her third son, who was born just a few weeks after her husband's death. But she returned with all three sons to work in Quito with Marj.

Olive Fleming had spent only two months in Ecuador when her husband died. She waited for God's leading.

Johnny Keenan continued the gift drops, and thousands of prayers from all over the world wafted over the dark jungles of the Aucas. Nate Saint's sister, Rachel, continued to study the Auca language with the help of Dayuma.

But the words *I must go* continued to echo in Elisabeth Elliot's heart. It was beyond belief that she longed to go to the very savages who had killed her husband!

Less than 3 years later, Elisabeth was in a tiny leaf-thatched hut not many miles from Palm Beach. In another hut, a few feet away, sat two of the seven men who had killed her husband. Several more Aucas were nearby. Gikita, one of the killers, was helping three-year-old Valerie roast a plantain.

What happened to bring this miracle about?

The year before, two Auca women had come to a Quichua Indian settlement. Elisabeth went immediately to meet them. One of them, Mintaka, was one of the two women who had stepped out of the jungle that day at Palm Beach.

The two women went back to Elisabeth's station with her. Elisabeth studied their language and prayed as always—to be able to go to their tribe.

Later Elisabeth and the two Auca women visited with Rachel Saint and Dayuma. The three Auca women were happily reunited after more than 12 years. The three talked about "going home"—which they did.

They remained at home for three weeks and told their tribesmen of the kind strangers and the love they had for them. When the three returned, they brought with them seven more Aucas. They also brought an invitation for Rachel and Elisabeth to come and live with them!

So on October 8, 1958, Rachel, Elisabeth, and Valerie went to Auca territory to live. The Indians received them as sisters. They built houses for them and shared food with them.

They told the women they had killed the missionaries because they thought they were cannibals. They knew they had made a mistake and were sorry.

God worked through all these unbelievable circumstances. Today these Indians are no longer called Aucas, which means "naked" and "savage." They are now called Waorani. Many are now Christians. The New Testament has been translated into their language.

The story lives on, even decades after the killings because God used the sacrifices of five who literally followed His leading even unto death.

His Son did that, too.

Both stories are beyond belief.

DEBORAH ON THE PLAINS OF PALESTINE

In *Women of the Old Testament*, Abraham Kuyper describes Deborah as the Jeanne d'Arc of Israel.[3] For sure, no country needed a Jeanne d'Arc any more than Israel did.

Israel fell into idolatry "frequently, rapidly, and profoundly."[4] They made it through such downfalls and rose again only by God's hand.

God gave Deborah to Israel during one of those downfalls. We find her story in chapters 4 and 5 of Judges.

Deborah's time on the plains of Palestine was under the rule of the Canaanites. Their king, Jabin, had an unbelievable army with 900 chariots of iron. Israel's infantry was ground down like fodder under those iron wheels. So those dwelling on the plains paid tribute to Jabin and were virtually slaves.

Only those who lived in the hill country were safe from the merciless chariots. Besides their natural protection (chariots don't operate very well in the hills), they also had courageous hearts. No doubt Deborah was an encouragement to them.

Deborah was one who could inspire the people to hope, to believe. She was the wife of Lapidoth, and she lived under the palm tree between Ramah and Bethel.

Deborah possessed both intellect and common sense. God had also given her the gift of prophecy and the talent of song.

Using all of her abilities, she had called the hill people back to God. She reminded them of Egypt and Sinai. She prophesied of better times in the future.

Deborah was also a judge who was fair and just. Her opinions were well respected. Her reputation grew as her songs were passed from one person to another and from hill to hill.

Along with a military leader, Barak, she built an army using guerilla warfare. The army was ready and able to fight effectively.[5]

However, the fourth chapter of Judges paints a realistic picture of Israel's condition:

"The sons of Israel again did evil in the sight of the Lord" (Judg. 4:1 NASB).

"And the Lord sold them into the hand of Jabin King of Canaan. . . . The commander of his army was Sisera" (Judg. 4:2).

"Then the people of Israel cried to the Lord for help" (Judg. 4:3).

For 20 years Israel had suffered at the hands of the Canaanites. Deborah, with God's leading, called for Barak. She told him that God commanded him, "Go, take with you ten thousand men of Naphtali and Zebulun and lead the way to Mount Tabor. I will lure Sisera, the commander of Jabin's army, with his chariots and his troops to the Kishon River and give him into your hands" (Judg. 4:6–7).

So God called Barak and even gave him the battle plan. But Barak hesitated. He said to Deborah, "If you go with me, I will go; but if you don't go with me, I won't go" (Judg. 4:8).

Some have said that Barak showed cowardice. But others say his request for Deborah to go was a request for the presence of God.

Deborah assured Barak that she would indeed go with him. It was absolutely unprecedented that a woman would lead the army of the Lord! However, Deborah knew that she had to go.

She warned Barak, however, that he would not be the honored victor if she went. She said, "The Lord will hand Sisera over to a woman" (Judg. 4:9).

Deborah is not the woman who took care of Sisera. It was Jael—who has a story of her own!

As the Lord commanded, the battle went on until all the men of Sisera fell by the sword—except for Sisera himself, who ran for his life. He ran to the wrong place, however, into the tent of Jael. Because her husband, Heber, was a Kenite and because Jabin, the king of the Canaanites, was friends with the Kenites, Sisera thought he was home free. Jael covered up Sisera as if to hide him. But her next move was to pick up a tent peg and a hammer, then drive the peg through his head.

After the deed was done, here comes Barak. He's ready to finish off Sisera. He may have hesitated at first, but fresh from his total victory over the troops, he is out to find Sisera and total glory! He enters Jael's tent and finds the five-star general pinned to the ground and already dead. So much for this "David" killing this "Goliath!"

Following the story of the battle, which is told in narrative form, comes the song of Deborah in the fifth chapter of Judges. Deborah's song is an ode to God's victory. It also praises some of the main players in the story. It was probably her number one hit.

Barak sang with Deborah. It was surely not difficult for him to sing praises to God. But when the song continued with "I, Deborah, arose" (Judg. 5:7), the words may have stuck in his throat! By the time the song reached Jael's part in verse 24, Barak may have slunk home!

The song of Deborah praised God and gave Him the glory. But the song also let it be known that God accomplished what He did through the women, Deborah and Jael.

Deborah was mighty because the Spirit of the Lord moved, qualified, and inspired her.

And, beyond belief, she had to go!

Wana Ann Fort in the African Bush

From the very beginning Wana Ann Fort wanted to excel. She started school at 6 years old and loved it. God had given her an ability to learn and she knew He expected her best.

She gave her heart to the Lord when she was 13 years old in a little Baptist church in Harrisonburg, Louisiana. At that time, she promised to do whatever He wanted her to do.

Wana Ann loved Girls' Auxiliary (the WMU® organization that was the forerunner of Girls in Action® and younger Acteens®). She learned about the needs of the world. She promised that she would go wherever the Lord wanted her to go.

Wana Ann finished high school at the top of her class and was valedictorian. She went to Louisiana Tech, working her way through. She loved college and worked hard. She also discovered the Baptist Student Union (BSU) and was challenged by it.

In 1943 the BSU planned to go to Student Week at Ridgecrest, the Baptist conference center in North Carolina. Wana Ann longed to go. Somehow she knew that if she went, she would discover what God wanted her to do.

Miraculously, overcoming the financial challenge, she did go to Ridgecrest! After much praying and struggling, she found God's answer. He wanted her to be a medical missionary.

No! Absolutely no! She went up into the mountains and told God all the reasons she could not be a missionary doctor:

1. She didn't have the money for medical school.
2. Her dad didn't believe in women doctors.
3. He wouldn't even want her to be a missionary.
4. She didn't want to be single (women doctors surely didn't marry!)
5. She didn't want to take all that biology and chemistry.

God dismissed her reasons and gave her Psalm 37:5: "Commit thy way unto the Lord. . . . He shall bring it to pass" (KJV).

Finally, Wana Ann surrendered. "Lord, You'll have to do it. I can't. But I'm ready for You to bring it to pass." She went back to a staggering schedule that still included BSU.

At her college church in Ruston, she gave her testimony, but her pastor did not think she had really been called of God. That spring at the state BSU retreat she was asked to give her testimony. Years later, one of the college directors told her that during a break various directors and other program people had talked about how sad it was that a young, misguided person like her had been permitted to speak!

The BSU had a big party that fall. The party was to welcome new students. One of those new students was a sailor in the V-12 program from Texas A&M University. His name was Giles Fort, and he was a medical missions volunteer! In four months they were engaged. (One down, four to go!)

In February, Giles left to attend midshipman's school and from there he went to the Pacific war zone. They agreed to wait for each other and planned to go to Baylor Medical School together.

Wana Ann graduated from Louisiana Tech in three years with top honors. She applied to Baylor. They notified her that they were taking no out-of-state students, all things being considered and all things being equal.

Wana Ann prayed about it and decided all things weren't equal. She wrote back expressing this and telling of God's call. She was accepted.

After a year of hard study at medical school, she welcomed Giles home in June 1946. A few days later, they were married.

God provided for the young couple. They were healthy and they had good jobs in addition to Giles's GI benefits. They finished medical school without borrowing a penny.

After internship and residency, they still felt the compelling call to missions. In 1952 they were appointed by the Southern Baptist Foreign Mission

Board (now International Mission Board). They also welcomed their first son, Milton Giles Fort III, that year.

They were asked to consider doing pioneer missions in Rhodesia (now Zimbabwe). Almost immediately they knew that was the place!

Southern Baptists had leased 150 acres in the center of the vast Sanyati Reserve. When Giles and Wana Ann arrived in 1953, they practiced medicine there in a little two-room mud-and-pole building with a tin roof.

During their 35 years at Sanyati, they saw the little mud building replaced by an outpatient clinic, an eye clinic, a laboratory, a pharmacy, an obstetrical block, an isolation block, a chapel, a boarding school, and missionary houses. Their family was building, as well. Four more brothers joined Giles III.

The Forts saw many healed physically, and they helped many find the Lord Jesus as their personal Savior. But some at home in the US continued to scoff. When the Forts came home on their first furlough, one of Giles's uncles said something about their staying in the States after serving their time overseas. Wana Ann told him that they were committed to a lifetime of service. He said, "Wana Ann, I always knew Giles didn't have much sense, but I thought he married someone a lot smarter than that!"

Both Wana Ann's father and his brother were sure that in Africa they were throwing away all those years of training, when they could have made a lot of money and amounted to something in the US.

In 1980 Giles, Wana Ann, and two of their sons were on the program of the Southern Baptist Convention. Her dad's brother-in-law, who was a retired Baptist pastor, called. He told Wana Ann that he was amazed they were on the SBC program. He said,

"Wana Ann, I never thought anything worthwhile would ever come out of those Catahoula hills!" (Harrisonburg is in the Catahoula Parrish in Louisiana).

Wana Ann declares, "Only God saw in a little country girl what He could do if her life were given to Him. He continues to use the foolish things of this world to confound the wise, so that everyone will know only He could do it and any glory that might come belongs to Him."

It is astonishing what God has done with Wana Ann Fort since she said, "Yes, I must go!"

LIANG OVER THE MOUNTAINS IN THE LAST FRONTIER

Old Wang, Little Wang, and Cai Wen had dared to cross the mountains to share the gospel with the Zhou people. During their introduction of the gospel, the mob's angry, screaming voices drowned out the story of God's love.

"The spirits of the mountains rule over our land! You dogs have been here only 500 years and you know nothing. . . . Now you want to steal our religion!"

Before the men knew what was happening, the crowd of farmers was attacking. They hit the Christians repeatedly with hoes and sticks. Even as Old Wang tried to protect himself from the vicious blows, he saw a particularly fierce young man hit Little Wang with all his strength, over and over, until he slumped, lifeless.

It took ten hours for the other two men to make the trip home on a creaking bus. Old Wang's broken ribs throbbed with pain with every jolt of the bus. Cai Wen was in even worse shape—eyes swollen shut, a broken arm, and bleeding heavily from his beating.

Oh, how Old Wang dreaded telling Little Wang's wife what had happened.

Old Wang and Cai Wen finally reached home and their wounds were treated. Old Wang wept as he told Liang about her husband's killing. He arranged for other church members to help with their farm, and to bring meat and eggs to her.

At church on Sunday, meeting in a home, the two men told what had happened. The little church had sent Old Wang, Little Wang, and Cai Wen to the distant village because there was not a single church over the mountains. And the people over the mountains had killed one of their missionaries.

Despite their loss, nothing had changed. Those people still needed to hear about Jesus. It was decided that Old Wang and Cai Wen must go back.

Then Liang spoke: "I must go with you."

That day the church prayed fervently for the trip. They prayed that the people of the Zhou village would come to know the Lord. Word was passed to other house churches, and they prayed and fasted as Old Wang, Cai Wen, and Liang started their journey.

The three rode the jolting bus for ten hours. It was dark when they arrived in the Zhou village. They stretched out beside a pigpen on the outskirts of town.

The next morning they walked resolutely into the village. Only two weeks earlier the villagers had beaten those who brought the good news.

Word spread in the village that the troublemakers were back. An angry mob gathered. Threats and screams filled the air.

Liang stepped out in front of the two men. "I am the widow of the man you killed less than three weeks ago. My husband is not dead, however, because God has given him eternal life! Now he is living in paradise with our God. My husband came here to tell you how you could have that same eternal life. If he were here he would forgive you for what you did. I forgive you as well. I can forgive you because God has forgiven me. If you would like to hear more about this God, then meet us under the big tree outside of town this evening."

The crowd quietly walked away.

All day Old Wang instructed Liang. That evening nearly everybody in the village came to hear Liang. She shared how God sent His Son to save a lost world, and they listened.

For ten days Old Wang taught Liang, and for ten nights Liang taught the people. On the tenth night, many of them trusted Jesus as their Savior.

Cai Wen and Liang returned home, but Old Wang stayed to teach and baptize the new believers. Two months later, Old Wang returned home with two leaders and a young man from the new Zhou church. During Sunday worship the two leaders expressed their appreciation to the church.

Then the young man stood. "I am the man who murdered Little Wang," he said. "The Lord has graciously forgiven me and I ask for your forgiveness as well. I, and our entire church, owe an eternal debt of gratitude to Little Wang and Liang for bringing us the message of life."

Four months later came more good news: the Zhou church had planted another church, two mountains over.

This story happened in a Last Frontier country where it is illegal for Christians to meet to worship in their own homes. It's against the law to start a new church.

All the names have been changed in this true story. There is no Zhou tribe. But every word of the story—which is beyond belief—is true!

A great band of lostness that girdles the earth is called the Last Frontier. The people there are in deep

spiritual darkness. Liang had to go and tell. Committed Christian women, is He calling you? It is possible
—and not beyond belief!

[1] Elisabeth Elliot, *Through Gates of Splendor* (Wheaton, IL: Tyndale House
Publishers, Inc., 1981), 47.

[2] Ibid., 104.

[3] Abraham Kuyper, *Women of the Old Testament* (Grand Rapids: Zondervan, 1961), 71.

[4] Ibid.

[5] Ibid., 72-3.

9

With Eyes Wide Open

$\mathcal{M}$y husband says that I see things differently. "Both of us look at the same thing," he says, "but you see it—oh, me!"

He's right. With my eyes wide open, I do see more. You know how people look at clouds and see a dog or cat? I see planting the flag on Iwo Jima or the wedding of the century.

I see a woman sitting in the airport and I imagine who she is and where she's going and why she looks distressed. My mother (who loved me) used to say I had a lively imagination. In defense of those of us who see better and who do have lively imaginations, we see the miracles! Yes, we do, and we are also the ones who can sometimes ask God to close certain eyes—and He does!

WITH EYES WIDE OPEN IN TANZANIA

August 5, 1995, is a day that many will always remember. However, six individuals lived the experience. It is something they will never forget because it was beyond belief!

The six who were involved included four Foreign Mission Board (now called International Mission Board) missionaries and two MKs (missionaries' kids). One missionary couple, David and Millie

Moreland, were serving in Kigoma, Tanzania. The other couple, Bill and Sandra Harrington, also lived in Kigoma where Bill, a physician, directed the Baptist hospital.

The Harringtons' ten-year-old daughter, Christine, was also along, as was her friend, fellow MK Joanna Giddens, who was going with Christine for a visit. Joanna was ten, also. Joanna's parents, Ed and Nancy Giddens, were missionaries serving in Arusha, Tanzania. They all had been attending a meeting in Dar es Salaam and were headed home.

Around 1:30 P.M., just outside Mikumi Game Park, they stopped for a rest room break between Dar es Salaam and Iringa. The area was open enough to see any wild animals who might want them for lunch, but had enough cover for a little privacy.

David Moreland takes up the story: "I went into the bush on the westbound side of the highway and Dr. Harrington crossed over to the eastbound side. A white Peugeot 504 with dark, tinted windows passed as I was leaving my vehicle, but continued on to Mikumi.

After I returned to the car, the two ladies and the two little girls went into the bush. As the ladies were returning, I saw the white car driving slowly toward us and knew immediately they must be the car thieves we had heard about. There wasn't time to take any defensive action, and as the car came to a stop, a man with an AK-47 jumped out and aimed the rifle at me."

Bill Harrington continues: "I was emerging from the woods to return, also. My knit shirt snagged on a briar, and that delayed me a few seconds. That providential snag was to greatly alter the events of the next two days."

As Bill was about to step out into the clearing, he saw the white Peugeot pull up and the bandits get out—with an automatic rifle—and abduct his family and friends. In that moment, Bill asked God for wisdom. He remained hidden as they drove away.

Bill ran to the road, and within five minutes he had flagged down another car. They began searching, questioning anyone they saw along the road. When the trail of witnesses ended, he realized the group had entered the bush. He knew he had to get help. He contacted the Tanzanian police in nearby Morogoro. He phoned other missionaries to come help with the search. In addition, he called his parents in the US to mobilize people to pray.

For the next 25 hours, the police, missionaries, and Bill searched what Bill believed to be the area where the abductors and their captives were. After that long, dark night ended, the enemy planted in Bill's mind graphic images of what might have happened. At that point, God gave 1 Corinthians 10:13 to Bill: "And God is faithful: he will not let you be tempted beyond what you can bear. But when you are tempted, he will also provide a way out so that you can stand up under it" (NIV).

Bill told God that he had reached the limit of what he could humanly endure, and that God would either have to increase his endurance or provide an escape.

"I received immediate relief from my foreboding thoughts," remembers Bill.

Now back to the abduction scene. David Moreland saw Bill drop to the ground after untangling his shirt. If Bill had been caught, no one would have missed the group for two days. God did give Bill the wisdom he prayed for.

Two other thieves joined the man with the rifle. They walked immediately to the ladies. Immediate compliance was the captives' only choice from this point on. The man with the rifle ordered David into the backseat of his own car and had him lie down across the seat. Sandy Harrington was pushed across from the other side. David's wife, Millie, and the two girls were ordered into the front passenger seat.

David raised up to check on everyone and the man with the rifle hit him in the face with the weapon. One of the men jumped into the driver's seat and drove in the direction of Morogoro.

"I began to pray," David says, "and asked God to cause other people to pray for us, even though they might not know the reason. I also asked God to give these men some feeling of mercy toward us."

The driver took the captives down a hunting road and drove into the bush. He stopped the car and made everyone get out and lie on the ground. He demanded their money and they gave him all the money they had.

The Peugeot drove up with the other two abductors. One of the men ordered them back into their car. They drove back to the hunting road then went deeper into the bush and stopped the car again.

Christine and Joanna were taken out, then Sandy, Millie, and David. They huddled on the ground together. One of the men said, "Are we going to shoot them together or one at a time?"

One man said something and another of the men took Sandy from the group and placed her in a kneeling position with her back toward them. He then put Millie next to Sandy, then David, and then the two girls, all in a line. They all expected to die, but a great peace settled over the little group. They experienced the presence of the Lord.

Ten-year-old Joanna Giddens said later, "I wasn't scared, though, because I knew that with God, everything would be all right. When they lined us up, we held hands, thinking they would shoot us with the machine gun, but we prayed for God to protect us with His angels."

Sandy Harrington says, "God comforted me with His words: Romans 8:38–39," which reminded her that nothing could separate them from the love of Christ—not even death.

David Moreland says, "I knew that when the bullet struck, I would simply step across a line from this life to be forever with the Lord. That assurance is more wonderful than any other possession I might have."

Christine Harrington says that when the thieves were ready to shoot, she "decided that would not be so bad. . . because I knew that I would be in heaven right away with my mother and one of my best friends."

Millie remembers, "I truly had a peace that passed all understanding. We were ready to go. If we died, we died, but at least we were together. We had surrendered everything."

David led the group to pray out loud as one of the captors stood Sandy up to shoot her. Then another of the thieves asked David, "Are you a *padre?*"

"Yes, I'm a *padre,*" David responded and explained briefly that he was a Christian missionary with the Baptist church.

The next thing they knew, they were all told to drink an orange liquid. David felt like shouting with joy! He realized the bandits were not going to shoot them. He had heard of other hijackings in which victims had been drugged.

David was given a much larger dose from the bottle of orange drink than the women or the girls. One of the kidnappers spread a large piece of cloth on the ground and told them to lie down and sleep. Then they drove off.

After the men left, David told everybody to stick their fingers down their throats and try to throw up. They all tried, but Millie was the only one to succeed.

Then they doubled back to the dirt track road to walk as far as they could before the drugs took effect. David walked in front. As he rounded a curve, he spotted his car with all the doors open. He didn't know if the thieves were still around. He hurried back to the others and they got off the road. Then the drugs knocked them out. It was about 3:00 in the afternoon.

Another one of God's wonderful miracles was that all five were unconscious throughout the night in an area that has lions, leopards, and hyenas—and they were not harmed!

No wonder—thousands were praying. The Assemblies of God in Tanzania were having an evangelistic rally in the Kigoma soccer stadium. Over 10,000 people were attending, and they stopped the service to pray for the missionaries.

The Kenya Mission (the organization of Baptist missionaries in that country) was having a prayer retreat. Many stayed and prayed through the night until the group was found the next day! Thousands were praying in the US.

All the bases were covered. God even got permission for missionary pilot Mike Cannata to fly into a military-restricted area.

When Mike went out to look for the hostages early on the morning after their abduction, he knew no other planes had been given permission to fly. It was up to him. He was overwhelmed by the immensity of the area.

He started praying, "God, there is just no way I'm going to be able to find these people today. You're going to have to show me."

A narrow dirt track had made an impression on him when he first came into the area. He doubled back to that track. African guides advised him to go another way, but Mike felt compelled to follow that little road.

"God knew where they were," Mike explains. "He just guided the plane."

Within five minutes God opened his eyes to see where they were! Mike arranged a rescue from the ground.

"That was a miracle. That was just the Lord," Mike readily admits.

All of the hostages agree. It was beyond belief!

WITH EYES WIDE OPEN ON THE ROAD TO EMMAUS

All of us have yearned for a word from the Lord. I've longed to see Him in a burning bush or to walk the road to Emmaus with Him. But if I had walked that road, would my eyes have been wide open or . . .

As Jesus had told the disciples, He had been arrested, betrayed by one of the Twelve. He had been humiliated by a mock trial, had been scourged, had suffered the Cross, dying for our sins.

But, praise the Lord, as He said, He came out of the tomb on the third day!

The women—Mary Magdalene, Joanna, Mary the mother of James, and the others with them went to the tomb (Luke 24:10). What happened is recorded in Luke 24:1–12.

The women found the stone rolled away. Two men in clothes that gleamed like lightning stood by them.

The men said to them, "Why do you look for the living among the dead? He is not here; He has risen!" (Luke 24:5–6 NIV).

They were the first to know! And when they told the Eleven, they refused to believe. Except for Peter— or was it really belief that drove him to the tomb (Luke 24:12)?

Next came an actual sighting of the risen Lord, recorded in Luke 24:13–35. Some consider this to be the most tender and interesting of all of the appearances of Jesus after the Resurrection.

The two on the road to Emmaus are Cleopas and another (Luke 24:18). Ironside states, "I believe this other was his wife." He adds, "At any rate these two disciples had loved Jesus; they believed He was the Messiah; and perhaps they were in that throng that watched Him die. Now, in deep perplexity, they were wondering whether He was deceived or a deceiver in presenting Himself as the Messiah of Israel, which they had believed He was."[1]

The two believers were walking along the way from Jerusalem to Emmaus. They were talking of things that had recently happened.

Luke 24:15 tells us that Jesus came up and started walking with them. But the two did not recognize Him. Jesus asked them what they were talking about.

Cleopas's reply amounts to, "Where have You been?"

Then the story poured out. Don't You know what happened to Jesus of Nazareth? Don't You know that the chief priests and rulers handed Him over to be sentenced to death, and they crucified Him? The two also told Jesus about the women going to the tomb, and that the women had seen a vision of angels who told them that Jesus was alive.

In his commentary, Ironside says that Jesus drew near to the two grief-stricken disciples: Jesus was there! "But they did not know it; they did not realize it, and I think oftentimes the same is true with us," Ironside states. "Sometimes we are going through trials,

126

bewilderments, sorrow, disappointments, and we feel
so utterly alone, we feel as though no one cares, but if
our eyes could only be opened—like the eyes of that
servant of Elisha . . . when he saw the angels of the
Lord encamped around them to protect them from
their enemies—we might have a similar experience."²

Those two on the road to Emmaus were not
expecting Jesus, and they did not recognize Him.
Finally, Jesus spoke. Don't you remember what the
prophets said? Didn't they say that Christ would suffer and die? Luke 24:27 says that Jesus started with
Moses and explained everything to them.

By this time they had reached the village of
Emmaus. They asked Jesus to stay with them since it
was nearly night. And He did stay. At supper, He
broke the bread and gave thanks.

"Then their eyes were opened and they recognized
Him" (Luke 24:31 NIV).

It may be that they saw the nailprints in His
hands. Something made them realize—"This is He!"
Perhaps they looked at each other in amazement and
when they looked back—He was gone!

The two disciples rushed to find the Eleven in
Jerusalem, and they told how their eyes had been
opened. For unbelievers, it was beyond belief. But for
those of us who believe in the Lord Jesus Christ, we
know He lives!

With Eyes Wide Open in Occupied China

Wide open eyes can be blind. How often we look
right through people and events? There are many
ways we are blinded. I believe God can close eyes to
help His children. He can close the eyes of the
enemy. J. Donald McManus tells of this happening
in his book, *Martha Franks: One Link in God's Chain.*

When the Japanese invaded China, their move was relentless, gobbling everything in their path. They reached the North China Baptist Seminary in Hwanghsien on December 11, 1941, less than a week after the attack on Pearl Harbor.

Classes at the seminary were in full swing when the Japanese soldiers marched onto campus. Martha Franks, a Southern Baptist missionary, and five other missionaries at the seminary were informed they were prisoners of the Great Imperial Army of Japan. They were marched off, and the soldiers conducted a thorough search of all the seminary buildings. They kicked open locked doors. They confiscated anything suspicious or valuable.

There was a storage room opposite Martha's classroom. The soldiers completely overlooked it. The student food committee had filled the room with wheat bought from local farmers at harvest time. It was enough wheat for a whole year. Yet, beyond belief, the soldiers did not see the door to the storage room. It was in plain sight, but, miraculously, they did not see it.

The students thanked God for His wonderful protection of their lives and of their food. Actually, they could have thanked God for closing the eyes of the enemy!

The six missionaries were under house arrest in the home of one of them, Dr. Charlie Culpepper. The soldiers thought the missionaries were spies, so they searched every inch of the Culpepper house. Every drawer was opened and all their contents dumped out. Every closet was ransacked. Except for one.

Every summer the Culpeppers tried to can as much food as they could. The food was kept in a closet under the stairs. Canning jars were valuable possessions!

As the soldiers meticulously searched the house, they inadvertently pushed a piece of furniture so that it blocked the small door behind which the food was stored. Throughout the six months of their internment, the missionaries feasted from their secret pantry. The missionaries praised God for lifting His hand in their behalf. And they could have thanked God for blinding the soldiers' eyes!

The Lord continued covering eyes in the market of the city. The Japanese had taken all money from the missionaries and the Mission, as well. Each week the Japanese authorities gave Dr. Culpepper a small pittance for food. The Chinese cook, who had so faithfully served, was allowed to stay with the little band. Every few days he put a large basket on his arm and walked to the city market to buy food. He would haggle over the price of a piece of meat or a quantity of vegetables.

However, as the cook made his rounds, Christian friends slipped items into his basket. The father of a young man Martha had taught in kindergarten had a candy store. Sugar was nearly impossible to find, but this man was able to get sugar because of his business. The candy man slipped two precious bags of sugar into the cook's basket.

Another day, someone dropped in a lemon. It had been grown inside the house! Martha took a small rosewood stand, placed a few lumps of coal on it, and then placed the lemon atop the coal. It served as their centerpiece on the dining table and as a reminder of the kindness of their Chinese friends. And before it was too late, it became a delicious lemon pie for their dessert!

Another of God's good gifts was meat. Two missionary families in Hwanghsien had kept cows so the children could have fresh milk. When the Japanese invaded, the missionaries were required to list every item they owned, including every animal. There were five cows, one of which was a young calf. On a cold winter night, a new calf was born, making a total of six. Immediately the missionaries decided to butcher the year-old calf. They counted on the baby calf growing quickly before anyone noticed. In this way, the cattle count would still be five.

At midnight the missionaries butchered the calf and hung the meat in the attic. It was frozen solid by morning. It is cold in north China!

When the man who usually milked the cows came the next morning, he did not "see" the new calf. He simply milked the cows and took the milk to the Japanese. So each morning, the cook went to the attic and sawed off enough meat for dinner and soup for supper.

As the weather got warmer, there remained a good bit of meat in the attic. The missionaries needed to save it because they had no idea how long they would be confined. They had a pressure cooker, but no one knew how to can meat. Martha suggested cutting steaks to fit inside the canning jars. So they got busy cutting the meat, cooking it, and preparing it to go into jars in the pressure cooker. Martha was busy frying some of the meat when a Japanese soldier appeared at the kitchen door!

The soldier sniffed the aroma of those frying steaks. "You are cooking beef," he said. "Where did you get it?" Before Martha could answer, the cook replied, "If you go to Lung Ko on a market day, you can sometimes find beef to buy."

Did the soldier not see that work was under way to fill those jars to be hidden under the stairs? He did not. God must have closed his eyes!

With Eyes Wide Open in Mainland China

Dr. James Belote was area director of East Asia for the Southern Baptist Foreign Mission Board (now International Mission Board) in the days before World War II. He shared this story to illustrate that God has a thousand ways of making a way for His children— if we have our eyes wide open!

Dr. Belote and a fellow missionary, Dr. Eugene Hill, were on their way to a very important meeting of the Executive Committee of the China Mission. They arrived at the train station to buy their tickets, but the ticket agent told them that all of the day's tickets to their destination were already sold.

Dr. Belote explained that their need for tickets was crucial. The meeting was vitally important and both of them desperately needed to be present.

The ticket agent then said, "Yesterday's train has not yet arrived. If you want to ride on yesterday's train, you could go today."

The two men exchanged glances and agreed to ride on yesterday's train.

So while a horde of people waited in the station for today's train, the missionaries went through the gates to find yesterday's train. They arrived at their meeting on time.

With eyes wide open, we see the Lord move in our behalf. He can do anything. He has said repeatedly that nothing is too hard for Him. I believe.

[1] H. A. Ironside, *Addresses on the Gospel of Luke* (Neptune, NJ: Loizeaux Brothers, 1947), 704-5.
[2] Ibid., 705.

Conclusion

AND HE SHALL SEND HIS ANGELS

The year was 1971 and the place was Uganda. The infamous Idi Amin was president. The 10 million people in that east African country had no idea that a reign of terror was beginning during which countless people would die.

Harry and Doris Garvin were Southern Baptist missionaries in Soroti, Uganda. They had five children—Harry Jr., Tamra, Kenneth, Deborah, and baby Rebecca. Harry Jr., the oldest, was 14 and away at boarding school.

In Soroti the biggest concern was with the Muslims and Hindus. They were angry at the Baptists because some of their young people had been won to the Lord. Some of them had even tried to run over Kenneth and Deborah as they were walking down the street near their house! Those were anxious days!

Harry had just returned from a long trip to Nairobi, Kenya. He and Doris had gone to bed. Soon 10-year-old Kenneth knocked on his parent's bedroom door.

"Daddy, the devil is in my room," he said. He could feel the presence of evil, and he was afraid.

Harry replied, "I'll go and pray with you." He went with Kenneth to his room and read Scripture passages and prayed.

132

Kenneth then said, "It's OK, Daddy. You can go back to your room now."

In the next room were the two older daughters— 12-year-old Tamra and 7-year-old Deborah. They had heard Kenneth talking to their dad. Tamra was afraid because she had not been reading her Bible every night when her dad had given her verses to read. She asked Deborah to turn on the light so she could read her Bible. When she finished, she asked Deborah to turn the light off.

With the lights off, Tamra and Deborah saw a remarkable sight—an angel was outside their window!

At first Tamra thought that it was Jesus coming again because He was very bright. In fact, His face was so bright that she could not see it. But then she saw that the figure had wings and was turning from side to side!

Then, in her mind, she heard a voice speak: "Lo, I am with you always, even to the end of the world."

Tamra said that the fear that she had always felt while living in Uganda left, and she began to sing an Atiso chorus, "Ejokuna Edeke," which means in English, "Oh, God Is Good."

Tamra called to Kenneth, "Come see the angel outside my window!" Kenneth called back that since his room was next to hers, he would just look outside his window. Kenneth got up on his knees on his bed to look out.

A few minutes later, Harry went to Kenneth's room to check on him. Kenneth cried, "Daddy, come quick!"

Harry said, "What are you doing, Kenneth? What's wrong with you?"

Kenneth insisted, "Come here, come here, Daddy!"

Harry said, "Tell me what's going on!'

Kenneth replied, "You're too late, Daddy. He's already gone!"

"What do you mean?" asked Harry.

"There was an angel outside my window!" Kenneth explained.

Tamra then rushed into the room saying, "Yes, Daddy, what Kenneth said is true." She told Harry what she and Deborah had seen. When she returned to her room again, she looked out and saw the sky filled with angels, blotting out the stars.

Harry and Doris never saw the angels, though they did look out their windows. However, they believe that Satan had planned harm for the family that night, and God sent His angels to protect them.

That's beyond belief! But the Garvins believe—and so do I!

About the author

Barbara Joiner has touched the hearts of thousands upon thousands through her ministries of writing and speaking. Known for her wit, her storytelling, and her unique way of viewing the situations that life brings, Barbara is always ready to open the eyes-and the hearts-of her audiences to experience what God is doing in the world. Her love for missions has been evident through her 31 years as an Acteens® advisor. Through this WMU® missions organization, she has guided hundreds of teenaged girls to discover how they can make a difference for Christ at home, on mission trips in the US and overseas, and throughout life. Another of Barbara's special loves is leading groups of young people to conduct migrant camp in south Alabama, which she has done for the past 33 years. In addition, she serves on the Board of Trustees for The Alabama Baptist newspaper and chairs the Board of Trustees for Alabama WMU. Barbara holds a degree from the University of Alabama and has also done graduate work in the field of communications. She and her husband, Homer, have two daughters and five grandchildren. They all make their home in Columbiana, Alabama.

Also by Barbara Joiner

The Best of Barbara Joiner (audio-cassette)

Count It All Joy

The Story of Martha Myers

Yours for the Giving: Spiritual Gifts

Available through WMU Customer Service, 1-800-968-7301 or www.wmustore.com.

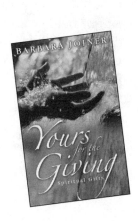

WMU
Discover the Joy of Missions^{SM}

P.O. Box 830010
Birmingham, Alabama 35283-0010
www.wmu.com

Thank you!

Your purchase of this book and other WMU products supports the mission and ministries of WMU. To find more great resources, visit our online store at www.wmustore.com or talk with one of our friendly customer service representatives at 1-800-968-7301.

WMU®
*Discover the Joy of Missions*ˢᴹ
www.wmu.com